A NEW BEGINNING I

Handbook For Joyous Survival

Jerry & Esther Hicks

We thank each of those who have participated in workshops and consultations with Abraham, for through that interaction this book has evolved.

First printing, May, 1988
Second printing, November, 1990
Third printing, September, 1991
Fourth printing, September, 1992
ISBN 0-9621219-3-2

Published by Crown Internationale
Manufactured in the U.S.A.

It is with great enthusiasm that we interact with you in this time. Not intending to do for you what you have intended to do for yourselves. Not intending to give you information before you are ready to receive it, and not intending to discover for you, that which you have intended to discover on your own -- but we interact as friends from your inner world who have agreed to participate with you in this time.

We are teachers, and we are here to teach Universal Laws that apply to all life experience -- physical or nonphysical -- so that you may enhance this physical life in which you are now participating.

We are offering you, here, absolute freedom. You see, as important as understanding the Creative Process, so that you may create those things that you want, it is just as important that you understand it so that you stop creating those things you do not want.

-- Abraham

ABRAHAM SPEAKS
THRU ESTHER HICKS

Excited about the validity, the power, and the clarity of the words of ABRAHAM — yet aware of a possible misunder-standing by the general public of the phenomenon that they were personally experiencing, Jerry and Esther Hicks began a rather tentative sharing of their ABRAHAM experience with a handful of close friends and business associates.

That was in 1986, and as they recognized the value to those who began to gather weekly in their living room plying ABRAHAM with meaningful questions, the Hickses made a conscious decision to begin to make ABRAHAMS' available to an ever-widening circle of seekers (those wanting and expect-ing enrichment). That circle of co-creating continues to expand — even as you are now holding this book in your hands.

ABRAHAM (they named themselves) a group of obviously highly evolved teachers — who are not currently focused in physical form — speak their comfortable knowing through the physical apparatus of Esther Hicks. They speak forthrightly to our level of comprehension...from their present moment to our present moment. Through this loving, allowing, stunningly brilliant yet comprehensively simple offering in print they guide us to a clearer awareness of the knowing within our "individual" inner world.

Contents

Introduction

How is your life governed? What part fate, what part by others, and what part by you?

Why were you born? Was it a quirk of fate, a decision by others, or was it by your choice?

Have you a purpose for life? And if you do, is it pre-destined, is it to fulfill others, or is it to serve your intentions?

What is the best use of the time that is left of your physical life?

What limits of bodily conditions, material conditions and relationships are yours?

What attracts those people, books and incidents to you -- of seeming magic -- that have such major influences on your life? And what part do you play in that attraction?

And, is there meaning or cause behind it all, or is it merely luck -- good, bad or indifferent?

Abraham will guide you to your answers to each of those questions that are directly related to your life today, and THROUGH THE FOLLOWING PAGES, CAREFULLY, PRINCIPLE BY PRINCIPLE, AND PROCESS BY PROCESS -- YOU WILL BE DIRECTED TO THE DISCOVERY OF YOUR JOYOUS DELIBERATE CREATION AND CONTROL OF EVERY EVENT AND CONDITION OF YOUR LIFE.

Esther's head was rolling gently, but erratically, as I looked up in response to her squeal of delight, "They are spelling the alphabet with my nose!"

That was November of 1985 and the "they" was a group of nonphysical beings who call themselves Abraham.

For 15 minutes, every day, for 9 months, Esther and I had been sitting to quiet our minds in order to learn, first hand, the identity of our "spiritual guides." We had been told that we would meet them through a "clairaudient" experience -- and here they were!

Joyous thrill bumps of confirmation covered Esther's body, and as the letters progressed from "L-M-N-O-P" to, "I AM ABRAHAM, I AM YOUR SPIRITUAL GUIDE, I LOVE YOU, I AM HERE TO HELP YOU"....we were elated!

Two months later, while we were lying in bed, her hand began to tap on my chest, and Esther exclaimed, "I think they want me to go to the typewriter," and they proceeded to type out the first of what now has amounted to thousands of pages of information.

And it was two months later, as we were driving on a Phoenix freeway, that Esther said, "I think they are going to speak through me," and Abraham's first words were, "This freeway is too dangerous...Take the next exit" -- and we did.

That was another new beginning for us, and I can foresee no ending to this truly fabulous experience.

I have lived a delightful, varied, rewarding life before this experience, but the years that we have had of this conscious learning association with our friends, Abraham, have been the most fulfilling yet -- and Esther and I take extreme pleasure in sharing our nonphysical friends with you in this manner.

Today is January 31, 1988, and Esther, my wife, has just now completed the typing of the words of the body of this book that has been dictated through her physical body by our delightful nonphysical friends, Abraham.

Abraham describes themselves as a group of beings who are living, but not in physical form at this time, and they are communicating to us, through Esther, from the nonphysical dimension in which they are currently focused. They say that they have lived thousands of lifetimes and that they are together, now, by their mutual intent.

"Abraham is teacher," they have explained, and by their choice, and by our mutual wanting and allowing, they are able to transmit their message to us, through Esther.

Esther, they have explained, is a sort of receiver/transmitter who receives blocks of thoughts and translates them at an unconscious level of her being. And in a similar manner she transmits our message, through thought, back to Abraham.

Abraham tells us that even before our physical birth into this life experience, that we had agreed to interact with them in this way, but they stress that the decisions that we are making, here in this physical dimension, are dominant and that it is our conscious choice to participate with them or to not participate with them. In other words, they will not speak with us without our wanting and allowing.

They began this book only six weeks ago, dictating a part of it each day into a tape recorder, and I cannot help notice the ease with which they have offered their part of this book, in contrast to the methodical way of my writing this Introduction, which we have agreed will be my responsibility.

I found that it was very difficult to define the beginning point of my "Abraham" experience, because each of my experiences has led to another which has led to the next.

I wanted to express the marvelous relationships that Esther and I share and the tremendous enhancement that our relationship with Abraham has provided. I felt that as you are beginning to read this book, you may be interested in the unfolding of the process of Esther's ability to speak clearly the words of this wise and loving group of beings, but it seemed that the more I wrote, the more needed to be said, until I had pages of material and much more than is appropriate for this Introduction.

And so, as I always do when we are working together on a project that involves the hearing or reading of any of Abraham's materials by others, I asked to speak with them about the appropriateness of my ideas in the context of their overall philosophy and their intentions.

Abraham spoke right to the point -- and their excited emotion was unusually high -- "What is your intent in this that you write?"

"Abraham," I said, "I want to write something that will encourage the reader to read every word of this wonderful book, in the order that it has been written."

"Do you have other intentions?" Abraham asked.

"I want the reader to understand that they, at this moment, are at the beginning point of a new segment of their life, and that from this stage, empowered by the perspectives that you offer through this book, that they can expect to move forward into fresh experiences and knowledge at an accelerated rate of growth -- AND THAT FROM THIS NEW BEGINNING, THEY CAN CREATE THEIR NEW WORLD EXACTLY AS THEY WANT IT TO BE."

As I spoke, Esther's eyes were dark, and her head was nodding gently as it often does as Abraham is listening intently.

"I want the readers to understand that you offer whatever degrees of wisdom that they are wanting, and that for those who are open to new thoughts and experiences, there will be much received. I want them to understand that past thoughts, or past lives, need have no power over present intentions and that BY A CONSCIOUS DECISION TO ALLOW NEW THOUGHTS, ANYONE, AT ANY TIME, CAN DELIBERATELY BEGIN A NEW EXPERIENCE, and that by consciously utilizing the Process of Creation, that you have offered in this book, they can deliberately achieve glorious new learning and spectacular fresh growth -- in this moment."

I paused for a moment, thinking that Abraham might be ready to speak, but they remained silent, as if they knew that if they didn't speak, that I would. I continued:

"This is not a book about the psychic, the occult, the supernatural, the paranormal, the magical, or the metaphysical. THIS IS A BOOK ABOUT THE PROCESS OF DELIBERATE PHYSICAL CREATING, ABOUT THE BLENDING OF THE PHYSICAL BEING WITH THE INNER BEING, AND IT IS ABOUT THE MEANS OF JOYOUS PHYSICAL SURVIVAL OF THE DRAMATIC PHYSICAL CHANGES THAT ARE

ABOUT TO OCCUR THROUGHOUT OUR WORLD.

"Abraham, your message speaks to the person who wants to be in control of every area of their life experience, and I believe that each person who is ready to receive that learning will be enthusiastic about their recognition of the validity of the material in this book, from the very first chapter."

Again, I paused, but not long, because my thoughts were clear and coming rapidly as I was excitedly explaining the value of Abraham's book to Abraham -- as if they didn't already know its value.

"Abraham, I want to bring some sort of clarity to the whole idea of nonphysical beings interacting with physical beings. There is such wide variation in the mediums of communications -- and in their messages. Some write, some use Ouija boards, some sing and dance, and some speak using the vocal apparatus of the person who is in physical form. Some are almost not intelligible, and yet some sound as clear as the physical speaker's regular voice. The state of trance varies, also, from a very deep unconsciousness, to what appears to be a state of normal consciousness. The list of differences seems endless. Even an understanding of the dimensions in which they exist defies us. And so, their value to us comes through what we are receiving from them. And again we meet with wide diversity. Some of the messages are opinionated and judgmental, others are lighthearted and chatty; there is traditional thinking, modern thinking, open thinking, closed thinking, brilliance, plainness, confusion, and clarity.

"Abraham, I want the reader to understand that they can know the value of that which they receive from these nonphysical beings by the way that they feel, and that whenever they hear or read words that bring them great discomfort, that they can turn away, for now, because those words are not for them, in this time, and that they can accept only what they want to hear, and each individual has the ability to decide what is wanted, for themselves.

"I want them to know that their life is not governed by fate and that it is not under the direction of another. I want them to know that their life is all within their control. I want them to understand why it seems that the rich get richer, and the poor get poorer, and why the better it gets, the better it gets, and the worse it gets, the worse it gets.

"Most importantly, I want the reader of this book to recognize that they are reading a workbook...a how-to book of life. This is not a book of entertainment. It is not a book of history or of psychic predictions of the future...THIS IS A WORK-BOOK THAT EACH PERSON CAN IMMEDIATELY PUT INTO USE IN ORDER TO CREATE A NEW BEGINNING OF A POSITIVE PERSONAL LIFE."

I stopped talking, almost tired from speaking excitedly for so long, and Abraham smiled at me, more through Esther's eyes than with her mouth, and spoke:

"Write what you have said to us. It is most appropriate for your beginning section of our book."

And so, I encourage you to read on, from this point, in the order that Abraham has offered their message in the following 15 chapters. In the segment that follows chapter 15, you will find a section explaining Esther's and my physical evolution to the point of meeting Abraham, and to the writing of this book.

We have also included, in the final pages of this book, a transcription of some questions and answers from a few group sessions which will be of great value to you once you have read and understood the principles that are offered in these first 15 chapters.

Jerry Hicks
San Antonio, Texas
January, 1988

FREE
INTRODUCTORY
TAPE

This limited 90 minute INTRODUCTION TO ABRAHAM cassette offer provides a stimulating overview of Abraham's basic message: The process of communication with your inner world, and the effective personal utilization of the Laws of the Universe in the conscious creation of whatever you want to be or do or have. And Jerry and Esther's explanation of their personal Abraham experience...To receive your free introductory tape, send $2.75 for shipping and handling and allow 1 to 4 weeks for delivery.

Send your order to: Abraham Speaks, P.O. Box 1706, Boerne, TX 78006

Name

Address

City   State   Zip

Telephone number: BIF92

Part I

1

Who Is Abraham, Who Are You and What Is the Value of Our Interaction

Dear Readers,

Within this book, you will find the key to your clear and DELIBERATE CREATIVE CONTROL of this physical life experience -- as well as the key to the JOYOUS EXTENSION of that physical life experience.

We are joyous here, as we gather in this nonphysical dimension, beginning on this day the writing of another book. And while this is not the first book that we have written together through this woman who is now taking dictation from us, it is, perhaps, the most significant that we have written together.

As we are writing this book, we are filled with joyous enthusiasm, for we are completing an intention that has been set into motion a very long time ago, and as with all things that are intended and then are allowed and received -- there is contented joy.

As we begin to put these words upon the page, we are filled with eager anticipation of your receiving of them. But, do not misunderstand, for we take no responsibility for your reception of these words, for as teachers, we have learned that we can offer information and knowing, but the receiving comes only by the decision of the one who seeks.

We interact with you, intending to be offerers of knowing and stimulators of thought, but it is not our intent to do for you that which you have clearly intended to do for yourselves.

As we begin, we will take a moment to explain to you who we are, that you might have a clearer understanding, not only of who we are, but of who you are. For a part of you, a part unknown to you, perhaps, is very much as we are now, in our nonphysical dimension.

We are wanting you to understand, more clearly, how it is that you have chosen this physical life experience in this time, what it is that you are expecting to gain from it, and give to it, and how this physical life experience fits into the broader picture of life experience. It is our intent to bring you to a clearer understanding of who you are.

We are a group of nonphysical beings who are currently living in a dimension that is different from the physical dimension in which you are focused. We stress that we are living, for we are not wanting you to assume that because we are not in physical form, that we are dead.

WE ARE VERY MUCH ALIVE -- AND WE ARE VERY MUCH INVOLVED IN LIFE.

There are many of us gathered together here. We are, what you would term, "a family", although we are not a family in the physical sense that you usually think of a family. If you were able to see us as separate beings, you would see us as approximately one hundred beings. Some of us have experienced many physical life experiences, and some of us have not. And while we are currently participating with you through this woman through whom we are speaking, we also are participating in other life experience at the same time, and, like you, we are working upon more than one project. We are not a family that has come together by birth, but a family that has been drawn together through evolvement.

Those of us who are gathered here are together because we are of the same intention, and just as you hold many intentions within your heart in any given moment, we do as well. And all of our intentions are compatible with the intentions of the others who are gathered here.

When we are interacting with one another in our nonphysical dimension, we do so not with spoken or written word, but with the transmission of thought or intent one to another. In our nonphysical dimension we do not call one another by name, for our recognition of one another goes beyond that which a label or a name offers.

As we offer these words, we are wanting you to have a clearer understanding of who you are and of who we are, but more importantly, we are wanting you to recognize your reason, or your intention, that came forth from your Inner Being at the time that you made the decision to be a part of this physical experience -- FOR IN UNDERSTANDING YOUR REASONS FOR WANTING TO BE IN PHYSICAL FORM, YOUR PHYSICAL EXPERIENCE WILL BE TREMENDOUSLY ENHANCED.

Perhaps you will come to understand your inner motivation, that feeling of urging that comes forth from within, that you, perhaps, cannot make sense of from your conscious thinking perspective.

Perhaps, many of the mysteries of your physical experience will be solved as you read this book, and perhaps you will gain a clearer understanding of what you are currently wanting to do, in light of the broader, clearer perspective that will be provided to you through the words that are written here in these pages.

We offer these words with tremendous joy, with tremendous excited anticipation, and with great love.

December 15, 1987

WORDS TRULY DO NOT TEACH. True knowing comes from life experience, and that is the reason that we are all continually engaging in life experience. But we offer these words, that they might stimulate your thinking, that through your thoughts, you may draw life experience that will bring you to a clearer understanding, or to more knowing.

TRULY, A TEACHER IS A STIMULATOR OF THOUGHT.

As we are beginning this book, we are seeking a beginning place, and that is not an easy thing to do, for each of us, physical or nonphysical, is at a different point of understanding.

There is truly not a specific order to learning or to growth because each of us, at our current point of understanding, or from our current perspective, set our thoughts into motion, and they attract life experience -- and from that life experience we draw our knowing.

You are a marvelous physical being, and you are dominantly focused in the physical dimension in which you dwell. Your physical perspective allows you to perceive only that which is of your physical dimension. We are not critical of that, for there is tremendous value in this physical life in which you are focused. And while you have lived many life experiences, both physical and nonphysical, you have no conscious memory of that which you have experienced before this physical lifetime, and that enables you to consciously remain focused upon this lifetime, and upon that which you are wanting to accomplish with it.

You are physical beings in this physical dimension upon planet earth -- because you have intended it to be that way. And as you are experiencing this life experience, you are fulfilling that decision that you have set forth prior to your physical birth.

That part of you who made the decision before your physical birth -- is still a part of you. We call it your "INNER BEING," for there are not accurate physical words to describe this part of you -- but it is a broader, wiser, certainly older you -- the part of you that transcends physical birth and death -- the part of you that is aware of all of the experiences that it has participated in, both physical and nonphysical.

One of the basic reasons that we are writing this book is to help you to recognize that your Inner Being exists. And that while you are, indeed, focused in this physical dimension -- that you may have access to the knowing that is held by your Inner Being, if you will allow it.

2

Creating by Deliberate Intent
— or by Default

December 15, 1987

Just as there is no ending to life, there is no ending to growth. For both growth and life are eternal, or everlasting. And while physical experience does have decided beginnings and endings, THE ENDING OF A PHYSICAL LIFE EXPERIENCE IS CERTAINLY NOT THE ENDING OF LIFE -- NOR IS IT THE ENDING OF GROWTH.

And while all life experience is growth experience, physical life experience provides an opportunity for a specific sort of growth that is available only through physical life experience. And it is for that reason, that each of you, in physical form, has so specifically and so deliberately intended, and wanted, to be a part of this physical life experience.

As you have made the decision to be here, to experience life, you have intended to understand, through this physical life process, the Creative Process, that you may **deliberately** create that which you choose within this physical life experience. It is your dominant intention as you are in physical form at this time.

And because that intention is of such importance to you, we are interacting with you, in this time, from our nonphysical dimension, that we might stimulate your thinking toward an understanding and application of the DELIBERATE CREATIVE PROCESS.

WE WILL BEGIN BY EXPLAINING TO YOU THAT YOU ARE THE CREATOR OF ALL THAT OCCURS IN ALL OF YOUR LIFE EXPERIENCE.

Because you are now specifically focused in this physical life experience, we will speak of the CREATIVE PROCESS as it applies to this physical life experience in which you are now participating.

You create your physical life experience through your thoughts. Literally, every thought that you think gives birth to a creation.

The thoughts that you think, regarding those things that you want, set into motion the creation, and eventual fulfillment, of that which you want. And likewise, the thoughts that you think, regarding those things that you do not want, set into motion the creation, and eventual fulfillment, of that which you do NOT want.

Regardless of whether your thoughts are in the direction of what is wanted, or in the direction of what is not wanted -- in the direction of that which excites you, and pleases you, or in the direction of that which you fear, which does not please you -- EVERY THOUGHT HAS CREATIVE POWER.

As you look into your life experience, analyzing it from this new viewpoint, you may recognize, immediately, how it is that you have experienced, and are experiencing, that which you have literally drawn into your life experience through your thought.

Every thought is powerful, and any thought that is brought to mind often, even without the presence of high emotion, will eventually manifest into the physical realization or actualization, but every thought is not equal in its ability to create, or in its speed for physical manifestation. The thoughts that you set forth in combination with great emotion are the most powerful of your thoughts, whether they are positive thoughts (in the direction of what is wanted) coupled with positive emotion, or negative thoughts (in the direction of what is not wanted) coupled with negative emotion -- the emotion that you feel as you are giving thought, propels, and brings into physical realization, that which you are giving thought to, very quickly. Any thought that is brought to mind often, even without the presence of high emotion, will eventually manifest into the physical realization or actualization.

To summarize this segment of the Creative Process: Understand that all thoughts create -- and the more emotion that is present at the time that a thought is set in motion, the faster the creation will be received -- and as frequent thought is given in any direction, without the hindrance of negative thought, there is certain creation, eventually.

When you fully understand what you have just read here, it will be very clear to you how it is that you have attracted the life experience that you are currently living, and as you look into your past, remembering that which you have created, you will recognize, without exception, that all of it has come to you through your thoughts.

When you are deliberately deciding that you want a thing, and are giving your conscious deliberate thought to it -- that is creation at its best, but when you are giving thought to that which you do not want, but nevertheless creating it -- that is creation by default.

We write this book with great enthusiasm because, from our perspective, we have observed that more of you, who are in physical form upon planet earth at this time, are creating by default rather than by conscious and deliberate intent, and it is our desire that we may stimulate your thoughts, as you read these words, to the point of understanding how it is that this creating is occurring, and as you understand the process by which you are creating, then you will have more possibility of being in deliberate control of your current life situation.

WE WILL STATE THE LAW OF CREATION IN SIMPLE TERMS HERE: WANT IT, AND ALLOW IT TO BE --AND IT IS. (Perhaps even a better term than "want," would be, "intend," for in the intending, there is wanting, certainly, and also an expectation for the receiving. "Intend" is a broader, more inclusive word) **We will restate the LAW OF CREATION: INTEND IT, AND ALLOW IT -- AND IT IS.**

As we observe your participation in your physical world, we are aware that it is the ALLOWING part of this equation that is out of balance for most of you. Many of you have long lists of unfulfilled wants, and although there is always room for improvement in clarifying precisely what it is that you are intending, as more of you begin to allow yourself the receipt of that which you want, there will be much more deliberate creating occurring, and as a result, there will be much more joy and contentment experienced.

CONTENTMENT COMES ONLY FROM INTENDING -- AND THEN ALLOWING AND RECEIVING.

Many of you, as you set a creation into motion, remove the possibility of its creation at the time you give birth to the creation.

For example: "I want a new red car, but it is too expensive." You see, you have given birth to your new red car on the one hand, and in the same breath you have removed the possibility of receiving it by your statement that it is too expensive. And much of that which you would create is voided in just that way.

The statement, "I want a new red car," is one half of the equation for creation -- the wanting or intending part. But, "It is too expensive," is stifling the allowing, you see. And so, recognize that you have only to state, "I want a new red car," and leave it at that -- not setting forth your counter-creation, your

18

contradictory-creation, your destructive-creation, your anti-creation or your un-creation.

OFFER ONLY THOSE THOUGHTS AND WORDS THAT ARE IN THE DIRECTION OF WHAT YOU WANT.

December 16, 1987

While you are physical beings in this time, and we are not, our life experiences are not so different as you might imagine them to be. There are laws which apply to our nonphysical experience just as they apply to your physical experience.

While it is true that there are many earthly agreements, that you are participating within that we are not currently participating within -- THE LAWS OF THE UNIVERSE REMAIN CONSTANT, REGARDLESS OF THE DIMENSION IN WHICH YOU DWELL. The Law of Creation is such a law.

Perhaps, the most interesting thing about a law is that IT IS whether you recognize that IT IS, or not. In other words, it affects you, even in your ignorance of it.

YOU ARE SETTING CREATION INTO MOTION THROUGH YOUR THOUGHTS, WHETHER YOU UNDERSTAND THAT YOU ARE, OR NOT. That is a reason that we are writing this book. We are wanting you to understand the Law of Creation, that you may, deliberately, apply it to the physical life experience in which you are currently participating -- rather than applying it "accidentally," or by default, because of your lack of understanding.

And so, what is, "creating by default?" It is setting into motion the creation of something that you really do not want, by giving your attention, or focus of thought, to it, until it is created. Much of what you are experiencing would fall into that category, would it not? The usual response when one hears for the first time, that they are the creator of their life experience -- and that all that they are experiencing, without exception, is by their own doing -- is, "How can that be? I would not have created this thing that I do not want."

We agree that you would not deliberately create that which you do not want, in most cases, but we will not agree that you have not created it -- FOR THERE IS NOT ANOTHER WHO CREATES IN YOUR LIFE EXPERIENCE.

It is not possible to create within the life experience of another. You cannot create in their experience -- and they cannot create in yours. Therefore, everything that you are experiencing is by your own creative hand, or more appropriately said, by your own creative thought.

As you are participating in this physical life experience, seeing through your physical perception, it is sometimes difficult for you to understand that your creating is not occurring out in the physical world. You believe that you do your creating by banging around in the physical world, but your creating occurs, without exception, within your Creative Workshop. You are the only one in your Creative Workshop unless you allow another in, or invite another in through your thought.

Of course, by now, you have already arrived at the conclusion, that if you are creating through your thought, that it is of extreme importance that you control your thoughts so that you may deliberately set into motion the creation of that which you choose. And in the next pages it is our intention to offer to you some exercises that will assist you in that very thing.

EXERCISE FOR DELIBERATE CREATION

THE FOLLOWING IS AN EXERCISE TO ASSIST YOU IN THE DELIBERATE CREATION OF WHATEVER YOU DESIRE;

It is best, in the early stages of understanding the Deliberate Creative Process, to target three or four of your primary desires. Eventually, you will be able to, simultaneously, create in unlimited directions, but as you are learning the process, it is best to focus in only three or four directions.

Select those desires or wants or intentions that are most important to you in this time, and write each of them at the top of a separate sheet of paper in this way:

"I intend to receive..." and then write whatever it is that you are intending to receive. And then take each of those sheets of paper, individually, and complete them, one at a time, as follows:

Below your statement of intent write, "These are the reasons that I intend..." and then restate your intention. And write all of the reasons that you want this.

Write what flows forth from you. Do not write what someone else wants you to want, but that which is important to you. Write as long as it flows forth naturally. Do not force it. WHEN YOU ARE WRITING, YOU ARE AT THE STRONGEST POINT OF FOCUS THAT YOU CAN ACHIEVE WITH YOUR CONSCIOUS THINKING BEING.

Then turn your sheet of paper to the other side, and write at the top: "I know that this is, (or 'that it will be,' if that stretches your belief a bit too far) for the following reasons...." And then state and write all of the reasons that you know that you will achieve that which you have written on the other side. Again, let it flow forth from you.

Once you have completed your statement of belief, fold the paper, and put it into your pocket or your handbag or some place where it will be convenient for you to retrieve it and read it during the day, and know that your creative work is complete. CONSIDER IT DONE! Realize that you have set into motion the creation of that intention which you have stated and written.

On the first side of your paper, you have stated your intention, and below it you have enhanced the wanting or the intending part of the equation for creation. On the second side of the sheet you have enhanced the allowing part of the equation for creation. And now, it is complete.

There is nothing more for you to do toward the creation of that which you have intended -- other than to allow it to be.

And by that we are saying that unless you create against the creation that you have set into motion, with your thoughts that bring forth fear or doubt or worry, or your notice it has not yet happened, then that creation will appear within your physical experience.

You see, as you are noticing that what you have intended has not yet occurred, what you are giving your attention to, is the lack of that which you want. And as you give your attention to anything, you create more of it. And so your notice that it has not yet occurred creates more of it not yet occurring. YOUR NOTICE OF THE LACK CREATES MORE OF THE LACK.

THE MORE INTENSE EMOTION THAT IS PRESENT WITHIN YOU, AS YOU ARE STATING THAT WHICH YOU WANT -- THE FASTER YOU WILL RECEIVE IT.

Be certain that you are thinking, always, in the direction of what you are wanting -- not in the direction of what you are not wanting. In the direction of the receiving of it -- not in the direction of the fear that you may not receive it. In the direction of the joyous expectation -- not in the direction of your noticing that it has not yet come.

And then continue this process with the remaining two or three sheets of paper, setting each creation into motion with this process.

And now, your creative work is finished upon those topics, Now you have only to think positively -- or in the direction of that which you want. Do not allow yourself to think negatively regarding these topics -- or in the direction of that which you do not want. AND AS YOU APPLY THIS EXERCISE -- YOU WILL RECEIVE THAT WHICH YOU INTEND.

December 16, 1987

It is not necessary for you to contain your thoughts only to those three or four intentions that you have listed earlier in your Exercise for Deliberate Creation, for there are many other things that you must also tend to in this physical experience in which you are participating.

When you are consciously concentrating upon the task at hand, you are not usually miscreating, or undoing a creation previously set into motion.

Most miscreating occurs when your mind is DRIFTING, or wandering, during those activities that do not require conscious concentration, such as driving your automobile or taking your bath or grooming yourself. Therefore, it is of value for you to be FOCUSED upon something at all times, for your marvelous CONSCIOUS THINKING MECHANISM is not content to be idle. If you do not DELIBERATELY give it something to think about, or to focus upon, it may be stimulated by thoughts or words or actions that surround you.

3

Recognizing Communication from Your Inner World

Every being who is in physical form at this time is currently receiving communication from another dimension, from an inner dimension, from their Inner Being. And while there are those who are more aware of the communication from within than others, and while there are differences in the way that it is received -- EVERY BEING IS RECEIVING COMMUNICATION FROM THEIR INNER BEING IN THE FORM OF EMOTION.

Your emotions are not from your physical world. They come forth from the inner world and are directly communicated to you from your Inner Being.

The advantage of receiving information from your Inner Being is that your Inner Being has a

broader perspective, FOR YOUR INNER BEING
HAS THE AWARENESS AND KNOWLEDGE THAT
COMES FROM ALL LIFE EXPERIENCE -- PHYSI-
CAL AND NONPHYSICAL -- WHEREAS YOUR
PHYSICAL PERCEPTION IS LIMITED TO THIS
LIFETIME ONLY. And so, as you are sensitive to
the communication that comes forth from your Inner
Being, it is of great value.

As you are feeling positive emotion -- such as
love, peace, happiness, joy, excitement, exhilaration...it is your Inner Being communicating to you,
in that moment that you are feeling the emotion --
your thoughts are in harmony with that which you are
wanting.

As you are experiencing negative emotion --
such as fear or doubt, anger, hatred, jealousy,
stress, guilt, anxiety...it is a communication from
your Inner Being telling you that, in that moment,
that which you are focused upon is not in harmony
with what you are wanting.

As you begin to recognize negative emotion in the early
subtle stages, you will be able to immediately halt the creating in
the direction of that which you do not want, and, at the same
time, stop the negative emotion that you are experiencing.

You see, the Law of Creation is this: As you
intend it and allow it to be -- it is. THAT WHICH
YOU INTEND, OR WANT, IS POSITIVE, AND
THAT WHICH YOU DO NOT WANT IS NEGATIVE.

As you are setting forth a positive thought of
that which you want, and you are, at the same time,
experiencing positive emotion -- you are, in that moment, in the perfect position for the receiving, or the
deliberate creating, of that which you are giving
thought to. And the higher the intensity of the emotion -- the faster the creating will occur.

In the same way, as you are giving thought to that which
you are not wanting, and in the same moment experiencing fear
or doubt or any negative emotion, in that moment you are in the
perfect position -- having negative thought and negative emotion

-- to create that very thing that you are <u>not</u> wanting. **It is law.**
IN SHORT -- YOU GET WHAT YOU THINK ABOUT, WHETHER YOU WANT IT OR NOT -- AND THE EMOTION THAT YOU ARE FEELING AS YOU ARE THINKING IT, PROPELS IT.

December 17, 1987

In order to create anything that you are wanting or desiring or intending, you have only to set forth a clear deliberate thought of intent -- and then to ALLOW it to be.
Unless you are deliberately suppressing your wanting, because you have wanted and not received for such a long time that you have given up on your wanting, then being ineffective at the wanting part of the equation is not usually what is keeping you from deliberate creation.
It is that you do not allow because you do not believe. What you believe regarding anything that you want is extremely important -- FOR YOU WILL ALLOW ONLY WITHIN THE BOUNDARIES OF YOUR BELIEFS. And for that reason in many cases your beliefs must be altered to harmonize with your intentions.
When you understand that your beliefs, also, are creations, set into motion by you because of previous experience, then you realize that your beliefs are not unchangeable, but, instead, they are pliable and moldable.
You alter your beliefs by applying new, or additional, thoughts to those beliefs until you have molded them into that which you now prefer.
There are limitless beliefs that are stored within your conscious thinking physical being. Most of them are dormant, and will remain dormant, but as you make a statement of intent, your beliefs that are within you regarding that subject will surface immediately.
Once one of your beliefs has surfaced, that belief, or thought -- FOR A BELIEF IS NOTHING MORE THAN A THOUGHT THAT YOU HAVE

THOUGHT BEFORE, THAT YOU CONTINUE TO THINK -- that thought will attract other thoughts that are like it. It is what we call the "LAW OF AT-TRACTION":

It is of great value for you to understand the **Law of Attraction**, for it is not your friend, or your enemy, it just is. It will attract more of whatever you are thinking to you. As you are thinking in the direction of that which is wanted, or that which you may term a positive thought -- the **Law of Attraction** will bring to you more thoughts that are in harmony with that, and as you are considering or pondering that which you do not want -- the **Law of Attraction** will, in the same way, bring to you other negative thoughts that will enhance the original thought.

THAT WHICH IS LIKE UNTO ITSELF IS DRAWN.

Most thoughts, particularly those that are not surrounded by high emotion, are not powerful enough to instantly, or even quickly, manifest into a physical equivalent, but as a thought, by the **Law of Attraction**, attracts other thoughts like itself, eventually that thought does become powerful enough to manifest into the physical equivalent.

It is of great advantage to give much concentrated thought in the direction of those things that you want -- and to give little or no thought toward those things that you do not want.

A fleeting thought regarding a negative subject will not harm you -- but DWELLING upon it will eventually bring the creation of it into your experience. Unless you invite that which you do not want into your experience by giving thought to it, you will not attract unwanted experiences.

When you effectively utilize the marvelous GUIDANCE SYSTEM that comes forth from your Inner Being -- in the form of emotion -- then you will be in a position to always effectively create that which you want, while you deliberately avoid creating that which you do not want.

As you are sensitive to the emotion that you are feeling, in any time, you will know, in that moment, if you are creating toward, or away from, that which you want.

YOU MAY TRUST YOUR INNER GUID-
ANCE, for it comes forth from that broader, wiser
part of yourself that has the advantage of knowledge
that is accumulated from thousands of lifetimes, both
physical and nonphysical.

BELIEF BRIDGING EXERCISE

HERE IS THE TECHNIQUE FOR CONTIN-
UAL, DELIBERATE, POSITIVE CREATION;

As you are moving through your day, participating in the
wide variety of activities which make up your physical experience -- BE SENSITIVE TO THE WAY THAT YOU
ARE FEELING. As long as you are feeling positive
emotion, know that you are creating toward those
things that you are wanting, but if you feel negative
emotion -- fear, doubt, anxiety, stress, anger, guilt,
loneliness, jealousy...stop, immediately, in the moment that you recognize that you are feeling the emotion, and ask yourself what thought or word or action
brought forth that emotion. And if you will respond in the
moment that you are feeling the emotion, you will, very quickly,
be able to identify what thought, word or action has brought it
forth, for as you recall it, the negative emotion will be intensified.

As soon as you identify what thought, word or
action has brought forth your negative emotion, ask
yourself, "What is it that I want?" Make your positive statement of what it is that you want. And then
make strong statements that will lead you from your
current state of negative thought and negative emotion to your desired state of positive thought. We
will call it building a bridge from where you are to
where you are wanting to be.

Do not try to build a very long span (or bridge) for your
conscious thinking mind will resist that. It has had enough life
experience that it is not so "gullible" as to make a very wide
jump, but if you will take small spans, making one statement

after another, you will find yourself arriving at the positive position that you are wanting -- and you will find yourself feeling positive emotion at the same time.

Once you have made the transition, from negative thought and negative emotion to positive thought and positive emotion -- you will then be creating in the direction of that which you are wanting.

Here is an example of the bridging process that we have just spoken about: You have begun this day by writing upon your separate pages those dominant intentions that you are currently holding, and among them you have intended to acquire a new red car. You have been very specific about your car, and as you made your list of what you want, and why you want it, visualizing yourself as the owner of this car, you felt yourself filled with strong, positive, excited emotion. And as you are moving through your day, thinking about various things, YOUR CAR IS ON ITS WAY TO YOU, for you have set it into motion, and you have done nothing to stop its motion toward you. And then, as you are driving, not focused or thinking about anything in particular, you see an automobile very much like the one that you are wanting, driving next to you. As you look over at it, if you feel happy or excited, that positive emotion is an indication to you that, in that moment, the thoughts that you are thinking, regarding the creation of your new red car, are in harmony. But, if, as you look over at that car, you feel depressed, or dissatisfied, or you are unhappy and anxious because you do not have it yet, or you feel jealous that the other driver does have it and you do not -- then know that the negative emotion is an indication that you are creating against your desire, and in the time that you are feeling those negative emotions, you are pushing your car away rather than attracting it to you.

Because you are sensitive to the negative emotion that you feel, you are now AWARE that you are pushing your car away. You may stop that negative creating, immediately, by bringing yourself from your negative thought and negative emotion to positive thought and positive emotion by building the following bridge:

"I want a new red car, like that one. By making this statement of intent, I have set the creation in motion. Now I have only to allow it to be, and it will be. My Guidance System has alerted me that, for a moment, I was pushing the car away, but I have stopped that now and am again attracting it by my strong desire. It is a beautiful car. I am excited when I think about having and driving my new red car. Circumstances or events or others cannot prevent me from having my red car. Only my own thoughts might push it away. But now my thoughts are again attracting the car. I know that, because I feel positive emotion."

As you begin to apply this exercise, you will get very good at it. You will find yourself responding to the negative "warning bell" emotion in the very early, subtle stages before other negative thoughts are attracted. You will have far fewer negative experiences experienced by you once this process is understood, for most negative experiences start out with a small and subtle negative thought and negative emotion, and then, by the **Law of Attraction**, blossom into something much bigger and more painful.

There is great value in recognizing, at the early stages, that you are upon a negative path, so that you may divert it, and by your deliberate decision create in the direction of that which you choose, instead.

Negative emotion is of great value, for it alerts you to negative creation. BUT IF THE NEGATIVE EMOTION GOES UNNOTICED, AND THE LAW OF ATTRACTION ENHANCES IT, SO THAT IT BE-COMES LARGER AND LARGER -- then your physical apparatus is damaged, and what is wanted is pushed away.

A very high percentage of those who are experiencing physical deterioration, or illness, in your time, are experiencing it because the "warning bell", or negative emotion, has been ignored.

4

Hindrances to Deliberate Creation

December 17, 1987

AN AWARENESS OF THE CREATIVE PRO-
CESS IS OF GREAT ADVANTAGE TO THOSE
WHO ARE WANTING DELIBERATE CONTROL OF
THEIR PHYSICAL LIFE EXPERIENCE.

From the broader perspective of your Inner Being, you
know that every being now in physical form is wanting deliberate control of this physical life experience. It is the reason, in
fact, that you are here. And as you are beginning to understand
the Creative Process, you may be filled with a very strong desire
to control all thought, that you may always create in the direction
of what you are wanting. Of course, that is DELIBERATE
CREATING at its best. **And here, we will speak to you
about the primary hindrances that prevent you from**

that constant deliberate control. And then we will offer an exercise that will assist you, tremendously, in that deliberate control.

As you are intending, and thereby creating, one of the most common hindrances is the INFLU-ENCE FROM OTHERS.

As you receive stimulation of thought from others, you may begin to think upon that thought, and thereby create in the direction of it, and the **Law of Attraction** will assist you by bringing forth other thoughts that are compatible with that thought.

Unless you are very clear, in every moment, you may be influenced by the thoughts or words or actions of those who surround you, to create something that you do not want.

The second hindrance comes not from the influence of others, but from the INFLUENCE OF YOUR OWN HABITS -- habits that have been developed at a time when your intentions were different than they are now.

When you are responding out of habit, rather than out of deliberate thought, you may be creating in a different, or even opposite, direction than you really want in this current moment.

Your thoughts are powerful creators, and your words are even more powerful than your thoughts, but your actions are more powerful than your words or your thoughts. In other words, every thought begins small, and by the **Law of Attraction**, as you ponder it longer or more often, it grows larger until eventually you will speak it. Once thought, and then spoken upon, you are led to action. And since YOUR ACTIONS FOLLOW YOUR DOMINANT INTENTIONS IN ANY MOMENT, it is very important that you are clear, at all times, about what your DOMINANT INTENTIONS ARE.

IF YOU DO NOT TAKE THE TIME TO IDEN-TIFY AND STATE YOUR DOMINANT INTEN-TIONS, THEN YOUR CREATING IS MORE EAS-ILY INFLUENCED BY OTHERS -- OR BY YOUR OWN OLD HABITS.

EXERCISE FOR DELIBERATE CREATIVE CONTROL

We encourage you to be aware of the natural SEGMENTS of your day. There are not two of you who experience the same SEGMENTS, for each of your life experiences are different, but we will give you some examples here:

When you wake up in the morning, the time that you remain in bed after you are awake is a segment. After you get out of bed, the time that you are in your house, making preparation to leave for work, or other activities, is a segment. When you get into your automobile, the time that you are in your automobile, moving from one place to another, is a segment. When you answer the telephone, it begins a new segment. When someone walks into your office, it begins a new segment, and so on.

IF YOU WILL RECOGNIZE THAT YOU HAVE BEGUN A NEW SEGMENT, AND AT THE BEGINNING OF EACH SEGMENT, IF YOU WILL TAKE A MOMENT TO CLARIFY WHAT YOUR DOMINANT INTENTIONS ARE -- WHAT YOU MOST WANT TO RECEIVE, OR GIVE, DURING THAT SEGMENT -- THEN YOU WILL BE IN DELIBERATE CONTROL OF YOUR LIFE EXPERIENCE.

You are beings who hold many intentions, and every intention does not apply to every moment of your life experience. Some of your intentions are more appropriate in some moments, while others are more appropriate in others. And it is necessary for you to identify which intentions are most important during which moments in order to be in complete and deliberate control of your life experience. For example:

When you get into your automobile, as you are buckling your safety belt, intend safety, keen awareness, perceptiveness of what other drivers are intending. Clearly, it is more appropriate to intend safety when getting into your automobile than when you are reading a book at home.

When you answer your telephone, take a moment, once you know who is calling, to intend that which you most want to communicate to that person. Intend clarity of thought and clarity of expression. Intend brevity if it is important. Intend to uplift the caller. It is more appropriate that you intend clarity of communication as you are speaking on the telephone than when you are swimming alone in your pool.

Most of you do not take time to think about what you want, generally, let alone thinking specifically about what you want, moment by moment, as you move through your day. But as you identify each new segment, and intend clearly what your dominant intentions are for that segment, you will have deliberate control of your life experience.

We are aware that it would be cumbersome to stop in every moment to identify what you most want, but it is not cumbersome to divide your day into segments and to take a few seconds in the beginning of each segment to identify what you are wanting.

In a short time you will find that it is very easy for you to identify the beginning of a new segment, and the few seconds that it takes to intend what you are wanting will not only streamline your life, providing much more time to do those things that you are wanting to do, but you will find much more joyous contentment within each day as you are receiving that which you have deliberately intended.

5

Intend Segment by Segment to Become a Selective Sifter

December 17, 1987

The physical world in which you are currently focused has evolved to a highly technical and complicated state.

Because you have the ability to receive communication and information, literally, from all around the world, you also have the ability to be influenced by that which is happening anywhere upon the face of your earth.

While technology allows you many advantages, it also brings with it the disadvantage of confusion and overwhelment, for you are living in an age of information overload.

Your marvelous CONSCIOUS THINKING MECHANISM is eager to participate in thought, and quickly goes to work upon whatever stimulation you provide it. And, in this time of technology, you are receiving tremendous amounts of thought stimulation to be sifted and sorted.

Because most of you are not making deliberate decisions about what is most important to you -- YOU ARE DEALING MORE WITH THAT WHICH IMMEDIATE THAN WITH THAT WHICH IS IMPORTANT.

Rather than tending to your dominant desires, you are bombarded by, and giving your thought and attention to, whatever is near you. And because of the technological society in which you live, literally everything that is happening upon your earth is "near" you. Therefore, it is more important now than ever before in the history of your earth that you take time, in every day, to identify, and state, clearly, that which is most important to you -- otherwise, you may be easily influenced to give your attention to that which surrounds you.

As we observe your physical world, we see beings who are going through the motions of life, performing the physical activities that they term "life," creating experiences through their thoughts -- but not by their deliberate thought. In short, for the most part, we see people who are living by default.

It is our intent, as we write this book, to stimulate your thoughts to a new awareness. To an awareness that you are the creator of your life experience, and to a wanting to be in deliberate control.

Until you have made a decision about what is important to you, ALL stimulation of thought draws your attention. And as you give your attention to anything, you begin to create in the direction of it. And that is the reason that there is so much value for you to break your day into segments and to intend clearly what is most important to you within each segment.

As you begin the process of Segment Intending, you will be in control of your physical experience, one segment at a time. The confusion that you are currently experiencing will lessen immediately, and instead of feelings of overwhelment and confusion -- which are negative emotions, "warning bells" -- you will be filled with exuberance and forward motion.

MAKING A DECISION, OR GIVING CONSCIOUS DELIBERATE THOUGHT TO THAT WHICH YOU WANT, PUTS YOU IN A POSITION OF BEING A SELECTIVE SIFTER.

As you decide what it is that you are wanting, the entire universe goes to work upon making that a reality within your physical experience. As you make no decisions about what is important, then you are not a selective sifter but a receiver of all things, and that is the reason for the confusion. Therefore, the more decisions that you make, in any day, the more selective sifting you will do -- and the less confusion, and the more satisfaction, you will feel.

December 19, 1987

Every being who is in physical form upon your planet at this time has intended, prior to this physical birth, to be in physical form, and to deliberately create, through the power of thought, by utilizing their conscious thinking mind.

As you have evolved upon the face of the earth, there has been much wondrous creation, and your creations have become more magnificent as you have achieved new perspectives with the receiving of each new creation. That is what evolvement is, wanting from a current perspective, allowing and receiving, and as you receive that which is wanted, you also receive a newer, clearer, broader perspective from which to make your next intention, and as a collective group of beings, who inhabit your earth, you have evolved tremendously -- even though the majority of you do not apply much conscious deliberate thought.

It is our intent, as we write this book, to stimulate more of you to want to create consciously and deliberately, so that you may understand that you are continually creating, and that you may choose deliberate creation, instead of creation by default.

AS WE OBSERVE YOUR WORLD, WE SEE THE POWER OF INFLUENCE FROM OTHERS AS A TREMENDOUS HINDRANCE TO YOUR OWN INDIVIDUAL CREATIVE THINKING.

It seems that you prefer to accept the creative thoughts of others above setting forth creative thoughts of your own. This is primarily due to your effective communication systems through your televisions and radios and publications -- for a very small percentage of your population makes the decisions regarding what is offered -- while a very large percentage of your population participates by viewing or hearing or reading -- and the result is that many are influenced by a few.

Every being who receives anything, does so by his own choosing. In other words, the information that is offered is not being thrust upon you. You are making the decision whether to receive it -- or whether not to receive it.

As most of you are not making a decision about what is important to you, you are not utilizing the value of becoming a SELECTIVE SIFTER, and therefore you are receiving some of everything that is being offered. And because there is so much that is being offered, and because you are not selectively sifting by making your decisions about what is important -- you are, for the most part, overwhelmed.

As we observe one hour of your television viewing, we are impressed with the amount of information and the amount of thought stimulation and the amount of influence that is offered in such a short span of time. And we are also aware of the effect that it has upon most of you. Rather than being clear and strong and exuberant in your motion forward, you are overwhelmed. Instead of making decisions about what you want -- that you may selectively receive that which applies -- you are bombarded with information, regarding all topics, to the point that you withdraw. While you are occasionally stimulated by something that is outstanding or more unusual, for the most part you have become numb to life experience, for it seems to be coming at you faster than you can cope with it, and so you literally close down, out of self-preservation.

We are writing this book because we are wanting to offer you a more joyous alternative:
BY MAKING MORE DECISIONS, IN EVERY DAY, ABOUT WHAT YOU WANT, YOU WILL AUTOMATICALLY SIFT THROUGH ALL OF THE DATA, ALL OF THE WORDS, ALL OF THE IN-FORMATION THAT IS COMING TO YOU -- AND THEN YOU WILL RECEIVE THAT WHICH EN-HANCES WHAT YOU WANT -- WHILE YOU WILL

6

Segment Intending: To Eliminate Negative Influence of Old Habits

December 19, 1987

IT IS OUR INTENT TO HELP YOU TO UNDERSTAND THE CREATIVE PROCESS, THAT YOU MAY <u>DELIBERATELY</u> SET INTO MOTION THOSE THINGS THAT YOU WANT -- THROUGH THE POWER OF YOUR CONSCIOUS THOUGHTS.

And it is just as important for you to understand how you are creating those things that you are not wanting, for there is a great deal more of creating by default occurring in your life experience than there is of creating by deliberate intent.

As you make a decision about what you want, you become a natural sifter, and THE ENTIRE UNIVERSE GOES TO WORK TO BRING ABOUT YOUR CREATION.

There are many variables about the speed with which it will come to you, for it depends upon the amount of focus that you give to it and the amount of emotion that you feel as you give the focus, and it also depends upon the other things that you are thinking about.

As you set a creation into motion, it will be -- unless you set other thoughts into motion that counter the original creation.

Those other countering thoughts come to you from many sources. Some of them, you dredge up from past experience, but many of them, you receive from those who are around you.

As you are absolutely clear, in each segment of your day, about what it is that you want, you will be a selective sifter, and you will receive only those thoughts that enhance that which you want -- while you will not receive those which do not.

It is important that you avoid the negative influence of those physical beings who surround you in your work place, in your home and in your social gatherings.

If you have decided what you want as you enter a segment involving another, and you enter into conversation with one who is speaking negatively regarding any of the subjects of your desire, you will have strong negative emotion, for your INNER BEING will be signalling to let you know that, in that moment, the words that you are receiving are not in harmony with that which you have previously intended. However, if you have not taken the time, as you have entered this segment, to identify your dominant intentions, then you will be more easily influenced by this negative conversation, for your "warning bells" will not be so specific, and you will not be as sensitive to them.

AT THE MOMENT THAT YOU 'HEAR' OR FEEL THE RINGING OF THE 'WARNING BELL', IT IS MOST IMPORTANT THAT YOU IMMEDI-ATELY TURN YOUR CONSCIOUS THOUGHT TOWARD THAT WHICH YOU WANT -- for in every moment that you are experiencing the ringing of the bell, you are creating in the direction of the thought that has caused the bell to ring, and you are moving rapidly in the direction of that which you do NOT want.

And so, the reason that it is so important to understand the power of the influence of others is because as they are stimulating your thoughts in the direction of that which you do not want, they are encouraging you in the creation of that which you do not want.

Of course, the easiest way to avoid the negative influence of others is to remove yourself, physically, from that influence when you feel the negative "warning bells" ringing, but it is not always comfortable to do that. Therefore, it is important that you remove yourself mentally and emotionally and that you give your conscious thought to that which you want and remove your attention from the conversation regarding that which you do not want.

Others may think that you are rude or uncaring when they sense your withdrawal -- but they do not understand the importance of controlling your thoughts, for if you do not withdraw, because it is more comfortable for you to remain than it is for you to disappoint your friends -- you will be creating by default.

Most of the physical beings who surround you are not in deliberate control of their life experience, for they are caught up in the influence of that which surrounds them, and they are not, at this point, willing to remove themselves from that influence, and to give conscious thought to that which they want.

WHEN YOU ENTER A NEW SEGMENT OF YOUR DAY, IF YOU HAVE NOT MADE A DECISION ABOUT WHAT YOU WANT, YOU ARE EASILY SWEPT UP BY THE INFLUENCE, OR EVEN BY THE CONFUSION, OF THOSE WHO SURROUND YOU.

As you get into your automobile, and as you intend safety, you will, literally, protect yourself from the ill wishes of others, or more commonly, from the undirected, unfocused confusion of those who are driving their automobiles around you. You see, when you understand the **Law of Attraction**, then you understand, more clearly, how it is that you attract one another into your life experience. Then you understand how it is that two beings, that are neither one focused about safety, are involved in an automobile accident. Then you understand how two beings, who are not focused upon health, are drawn to one another to speak about sickness -- thus creating it in their individual life experiences.

When you understand the **Law of Attraction**, then

you understand how it is that every thief is drawn to a victim. It is not by chance. It is not by accident. It is the **Law of Attraction**. And one who fears, attracts that which he fears. One who wants, attracts that which he wants. One who gives thought, attracts that to which he has given thought.

And so, as you enter each new segment of your day, make more decisions about what it is that you want, so that by the Law of Attraction and the Creative Process you will draw those experiences that you want -- and you will no longer attract those experiences that you do not want.

December 21, 1987

For the most part, creating by default occurs because you do not understand the Creative Process. HOWEVER, EVEN WHEN YOU DO UNDERSTAND THE CREATIVE PROCESS, YOU MAY BE INFLU- ENCED BY YOUR OWN HABITS, TO THINK OR SPEAK OR ACT IN THE DIRECTION OF THAT WHICH YOU ARE NOT WANTING.

It is not possible to create in the direction of your current intentions when you are acting out of habit, for your habits were developed in another time, perhaps when your intentions were different.

Many of your habits are tied to other beings that you are now participating with in this physical experience. You often begin to participate in conversation with others who are speaking in opposition to what you want, even though you now under- stand the power of your words, because you habitually speak with these people about these things. And rather than removing yourself, you remain, for you are not wanting to hurt anyone's feelings, or seem unusual.

As you walk into your house, out of habit you turn on your television set and sit and listen to what is offered.

As you hear words that are not in the direction of what you are wanting -- and you participate in those words with your THOUGHT -- you are thereby

setting into motion the creation of that which you are not wanting.

There are hundreds, perhaps thousands, of opportunities in every day for creating by default, and unless you have made a very strong and deliberate decision to give your conscious attention and focus only to that which you want, you will find yourself participating in negative creation many times in the course of only one day.

The process of creating hinges upon the intentions that are held by the creator. Before any creation can move forward, the intentions that you hold must be in harmony, one with another -- even though the intentions are different.

At any point in time, within your physical experience, there are many intentions present, and as they are harmonious, there is forward motion, and as they are not harmonious, there is slower forward motion, or no forward motion at all, depending upon the degree of disharmony.

Your thoughts are drawn to your DOMINANT INTENTION -- within any moment -- and as you are focused upon that intention, you are creating.

When you have not identified what your dominant intention is, your creative power is diffused because you create in many directions -- sometimes in many conflicting directions -- thus the feeling of standing still. But when you identify your dominant intentions, your focus and attention and thoughts will naturally be drawn toward them.

In short, what we are saying, here, is that you are drifting about; you are being drawn into negative conversations; you are responding out of habit to those old intentions -- because you are not making the decisions, in this time, about what your dominant intentions are.

ONCE YOU IDENTIFY WHAT IS MOST IMPORTANT TO YOU, AT ANY POINT IN TIME, THE NATURAL CREATIVE PROCESS WILL GO TO WORK FOR YOU. THE CONFUSION WILL BE GONE FROM YOUR LIFE EXPERIENCE.

Your Inner Being understands, very clearly, the **Law of Attraction** and the **Creative Process**, and it understands the process of the blending of intentions that takes place within you anytime you introduce a new decision. And while this knowing, at this point, may not be consciously recognized by you, you may trust that your Inner Being understands it, and therefore you may trust the emotion that comes forth regarding the thought that you are thinking. And as you begin to deliberately create in one area of your experience, you will have more deliberate control of all areas of your experience.

As you identify what your dominant intentions are, and as the natural process draws you toward focusing in the direction of those intentions -- you will be creating deliberately. And as you are sensitive to the way that you are feeling, the Guidance System that comes forth from your Inner Being will help you to stay focused and on track.

THE GUIDANCE SYSTEM, THE 'WARNING BELLS', THE EMOTIONS -- THAT COME FORTH FROM YOUR INNER BEING -- ASSIST YOU AS YOU ARE CONFRONTED BY INFLUENCE OF OTHERS, OR AS YOU ARE CONFRONTED BY OLD HABITS OF YOUR OWN.

7

The Key to Discovering Your Life's Purpose

THERE IS NOT ANOTHER CREATING WITHIN YOUR LIFE EXPERIENCE -- AND YOU CANNOT CREATE WITHIN THE LIFE EXPERI-ENCE OF ANOTHER. EACH BEING WHO IS IN PHYSICAL FORM IS AN INDIVIDUAL, INDEPEN-DENT CREATOR.

As you begin to get a broader sense of who you are, as you sense your TOTAL being, and not only your CONSCIOUS PHYSICAL BEING that you currently perceive, then you begin to understand that you have intended the life experience that you are living. Then you begin to understand how it is pos-sible that even before your physical birth, you were making decisions about what you wanted and about your purpose for this physical life experience.

As we observe those of you who are physical in this time, we are aware that many of you are searching for your life's purpose. You are wanting to know why you are here and what meaning this physical existence holds for you, but until you are willing to seek from your broader perspective, and not only from your conscious physical perspective, you will not find the answers to those questions.

You are here, in this physical life experience, dominantly focused within your physical world, because you have intended to be so, and we are not suggesting that you release your physical awareness and physical contact with this earth in order to seek out some other dimensional experience, but we ARE encouraging a blending. We are encouraging you to become aware of, and consciously, actively involved with, your inner world and your Inner Being -- for the blending will enhance the physical world in which you live.

EXERCISE FOR OPENING THE PATHWAY BETWEEN YOUR PHYSICAL AND INNER WORLDS

In order to sense your inner world, you must first quiet the physical world. In other words, you must remove your conscious focus from the physical world, that you might perceive the inner world. It is not a difficult process. It has been called many different things -- some call it meditation -- but regardless of what you call it, it is a time of quieting the physical, that you may sense the inner world:

Sit in a quiet place, making yourself comfortable, and close your eyes -- and be. Do whatever you can to reduce the possibility of conscious physical interruption. And as you are sitting, comfortably, quiet your conscious thinking mind. In the beginning that is not an easy task, for your conscious thinking mind is very quick to respond to the stimulation of thought. It is eager to participate. You have trained it to be fast.

As you are sitting, intending to quiet your conscious thinking mind, in time it will allow you your quiet time. We encourage a short time in every day -- FIFTEEN OR TWENTY MINUTES IS ENOUGH. The time of the day is not important, and it need not be the same time in every day, but it is important that you set aside the time, in every day.

As you have quieted your conscious thinking mind -- perhaps by concentrating upon your breathing -- and as you are not so aware of the physical world in which you live, you will begin to perceive the inner world, and for each of you it will be a different experience.

We encourage you not to compare your experiences with those of another, for there is no value in comparison. The intent of comparison is to find one better than the other, and as you are focusing upon the one that you do not prefer -- YOUR ATTENTION TO THAT WHICH YOU DO NOT WANT IS ATTRACTING THAT WHICH YOU DO NOT WANT INTO YOUR EXPERIENCE.

In time -- for some of you it may be in the first sitting -- you will sense a sort of numbing of your physical being, and that is an indication that you have succeeded at quieting your conscious thinking mind and your physical world, that you may sense the inner world.

What are the advantages of being sensitive to the inner world? When you understand that you are a much broader, more experienced, wiser, older being than your physical being remembers, then you will see the advantage of being in touch with that being, and, in fact, receiving communication from it. Each of you are already receiving communication from that Inner Being, in the form of emotion, but you can receive much more detailed information if you are wanting it. The process of quieting your physical world, that you may sense the inner world, will open that path of communication between your physical dimension and the inner dimension, so that you may receive guidance that is appropriate -- and that you may offer instruction in terms of what you are currently wanting.

You see, communication is not intended to be only from the inner world to the physical world but from the physical world to the inner world, as well. It is a pathway through which you may offer your clear intent. And once your channel, or pathway, has been established -- there are many wondrous benefits.

Once you have decided that you are wanting, or intending, to open the passageway from your physical dimension to the nonphysical dimension, then you have only to allow it to be. And the setting aside of the time in which to quiet your physical world is your allowing of the opening. And just as with each other segment of your day, it is important that you identify the intent as you move into this segment of meditation. If your intent is to open the passageway between dimensions, that you may receive clear communication, then state it as you are beginning to meditate. If your intent is to quiet the physical world, for you are wanting the relaxation of being apart from that which is confusing and overwhelming and tiring, then state that. You are the creator of that which you will experience during this time, but for our purposes here, we have offered this exercise that you may allow the opening of the passageway between your physical and inner worlds.

8

Your Connection to Each Other and to All-That-Is

December 22, 1987

We are continually seeking more effective ways to express our knowing to you, and as we speak of the Creative Process, it is difficult to put it into physical terms -- since the process extends beyond your physical perception.

You are physical beings, rooted in a physical dimension, and you are often wanting physical evidence to support that which you believe. And as we speak of PRINCIPLES that cannot be seen, and PROCESSES that cannot be seen, at times you are left without the proof that you seek. But as you accept that these words, regarding the **Creative Process**, are true -- there will be much tangible evidence within your individual life experience to support it.

It is our belief that as you read the words that are written upon the pages of this book, and as you evaluate the life experience that you remember -- and that you are currently living -- that you will see an exact correlation between the words upon the page and the evidence that you are producing day by day. FOR THE PRINCIPLES THAT WE ARE EXPRESSING ARE ETERNAL.

As you enter physical experience, you are surrounded by beings who have already arrived at many conclusions. They have created within themselves, many beliefs based upon the life experiences that they have lived -- or upon the stories that they have heard from those who surrounded them at the time that they were born.

As you are stimulated to think about beliefs that others offer, very often you attract life experience that "proves" to you that it is just as they have said that it is. FOR AS YOU BELIEVE THAT IT IS, IT IS, AND FOR THAT REASON, BELIEFS CHANGE VERY SLOWLY.

Rather than absorbing the beliefs of others, we encourage you, as you receive thought stimulation, to weigh it against the emotion that is coming forth from inside, and as the emotion that you feel is positive, continue the process of thought, and as the emotion that you feel is negative, release the thought immediately.

If you allow the "guidance" from your Inner Being to assist you, rather than listening to the varied opinions and beliefs of those who surround you -- you will have a much faster, clearer growth experience.

A being who does not understand the Creative Process, but who is excited about something -- will effectively create toward it. IT IS NOT NECESSARY THAT YOU UNDERSTAND THE CREATIVE PROCESS IN ORDER TO BE A CREATOR. All of you are creating in this time, BUT IT IS OF VALUE TO UNDERSTAND THE CREATIVE PROCESS -- IF YOU ARE WANTING DELIBERATE CONTROL OF THAT WHICH YOU CREATE.

As you look around yourself at all of that which is involved in your life experience, understand that all of it is by your creation, that every part of it, without exception, has been invited into your experience through your powerful creative thought. And while we cannot offer you the intricate details that are involved in this **Creative Process**, we will do out best, here, to give you a clearer picture of how your thoughts set into motion the creation of that which you are thinking about.

You are far more than the beings that you perceive through your physical senses and that you see in your physical bodies. EACH OF YOU HAS EMERGED FORTH FROM ANOTHER DIMENSION, FROM AN INNER WORLD, FROM A BROADER, WISER INNER BEING. And that being is connected to a group of beings that emerged from another group of beings, and so on. And while you are here upon the planet earth, in your physical body, living this physical life experience, you are, in a sense, a representative from much, much more than only one being.

As you have life experience, it is not only your personal physical being that is affected by it -- but all those that are connected to you. ALL OF YOU, WHO ARE IN PHYSICAL FORM, ARE CONNECTED TO ALL OF US, WHO ARE NOT IN PHYSICAL FORM, AND WE ARE ALL CONNECTED TO ALL-THAT-IS, and as you set forth a thought, literally the entire universe goes to work to assist you in the completion of the creation of that thought.

The Creative Mechanism, which is activated as you give birth to a thought, does not evaluate the rightness or wrongness, the positiveness or the negativeness, the goodness or the badness of any of it -- but it goes to work, immediately, to assist you in the creation of that which you have set into motion through your thought. It assumes that because you have set it into motion that you intend the receipt of it.

Your Creative Mechanism is always functioning. You cannot turn it off. Therefore it is of tremendous value to be sensitive to the way that you are feeling so that you may be guided to understand in which direction your Creative Mechanism is focused, for your GUIDING INNER BEING is not so indiscriminate. It is aware of the intentions that you hold.

And so, as your GUIDING INNER BEING recognizes that a thought has been set into motion that is contrary to what it knows you want -- it will give you a signal of guidance, a "warning bell," if you will, in the form of emotion. As you are receiving positive emotion, it is a signal to you, from your Inner Being, that, in that moment, you are creating toward that which you are wanting. When you are receiving a negative emotion, or "warning bell," it is a guiding signal from your Inner Being that, in that moment, you are creating in the direction of that which you are not wanting.

As you understand the inner connectedness of ALL-THAT-IS, then you are not surprised when that which you want, or that which you think about, is fulfilled. And as you come to understand this process, and to expect effective results from it, you will experience much more deliberate creating.

December 23, 1987

YOU ARE, FROM EVERY LEVEL OF YOUR BEING, JOY SEEKING BEINGS. You have intended, as you have come into this physical expression of life, to experience that which brings you joy, and which offers joy to those who surround you.

You are uplifters, participating here together because you are wanting to share with others the joyous life experience that you are creating for yourself. At the time that you made the decision to come into physical expression, you were clearly aware that you are the sole creator of your life experience and that each individual with whom you would be participating was also sole creator of their life experience, but you came to planet earth to participate in life experience with others because you also understood the value of being.

You see, as you are, you influence the thoughts of others. And so you intended to be in physical form to become that which you intended, that you might stimulate others to the same upliftment. From the perspective of your Inner Being, you joyously chose physical life, and you anticipated a joyous life experience.

As you pay attention to the way that you feel as you are participating in this life experience, you will know whether you moving in the direction of the joyous life experience that you icipated, or whether you are not. The joyous emotion that nes forth from within is a signal that you are in harmony with ...se inner intentions, and the negative emotion that you feel is a ...arning bell", or signal, that you are not.

If you are wanting to know about those who surround you, if you are wondering whether they are upon the path of their intent as they have come into physical expression, pay attention to the emotion that comes forth from within them, for it is not something that is easily hidden.

When you are a joyous being, it is obvious. And the joy seeking being is always drawn to the being who is experiencing joy. The Law of Attraction sees to that.

If you find yourself surrounded with joyous beings -- it is an indication that you are a joyous being, and if you are surrounded by those who are not joyous -- it is an indication that you are the same as that which you have attracted.

If you are wanting to offer joy to others -- then you must first be joyous. If you are wanting to offer health to others -- then you must first seek health for yourself. And as you intend and receive, there will also be contentment, and as you are experiencing contentment -- many will flock to your joyous example, wanting to understand how it is that you have achieved this.

It is wonderful that what you have experienced, to this point, in your physical experience, need not influence that which you __will__ experience, for as you are making your decisions, now, about what you are wanting, you begin creating toward those decisions.

You need not continue to experience a life of pain if you are now choosing a life of joy. But for most of you there is little change, for you usually pursue the same thoughts, the same other beings, the same life experiences that have brought you to the point that you are currently experiencing -- and as you continue to pursue more of that, you continue to create more of that.

IT IS NOT OUR INTENT TO GUIDE YOU

TOWARD, OR AWAY FROM, ANYTHING.

We are here to offer to you, from our broader perspective, from our point of knowing, the universal laws which affect the life experience that you are participating in. We are here to offer you our explanation of the **Creative Process**, that you might have deliberate control of that which you are experiencing, for deliberate control of that which you create was your dominant intention as you chose this physical life experience.

You are individual beings, here to create individually, and as much as you want to do for others, and as much as you feel a responsibility to create within their life experiences -- YOU ARE DOING OTHERS A DISSERVICE BY TRYING TO TAKE FROM THEM THE RESPONSIBILITY THAT THEY HAVE INTENDED FOR THEMSELVES.

December 24, 1987

What is the purpose of this physical life experience? It is a question that is often asked, and part of our reason for participating with you in this time is to guide you to an understanding of that purpose.

Your purpose, or intentions, were very clear to you as you made the decision to participate in physical life experience, and one of those decisions, or intentions, that you set forth from that nonphysical perspective, was that once inside of this physical experience, that you would consciously make the decisions that would set forth the creations that you would experience.

There has not been a path, or a track, that has been pre-laid before you that you are expected to find in order to fulfill your life's purpose.

It has been your intention to come into physical life experience and through the clarity of your decisions, in this time, to create the life experience that you choose. But as you entered this physical life experience, surrounded by the beliefs and the confusion of the world into which you were born, that clear perspective of your purpose has faded, and, in most cases, it has been forgotten, completely.

The very urging that prompts the questions, "Why am I here? What is my purpose in this physical life experience?" -- is coming forth from your Inner Being.

As you are existing in this physical dimension, perceiving with your physical senses, it is difficult to sense the totalness of your being, but as you begin to gain an understanding of your BROADER BEING, then you will more easily understand your reason for this physical life experience.

As you are understanding that you are infinitely connected to ALL-THAT-IS, then you understand the value of your representation upon this planet earth. For that which you learn through your life experience is not contained only within your individual physical conscious knowing, but it is expressed outward to other physical beings who surround you, and who participate with you, AND TO ALL BEINGS FROM WHICH THOSE PHYSICAL BEINGS HAVE EMERGED, and because all is connected to all -- ALL benefit from the life experience that YOU attract. Therefore, the evolution of your species is far broader than the physical evolution that you may be aware of.

As you chose to be a part of this physical life experience, you intended a lifetime of joy, for you were aware of the delicious nature of physical expression. And while all life experience, physical or nonphysical, is potentially joyous, there is a special and unique quality to physical life expression.

Your existence in this physical life experience is the manifested creation set forth by your intense desire. Your existence in this physical expression is a clear indication of your ability to create that which you want.

We are wanting you to understand that you are the creator of your physical life experience -- and that your physical life experience itself is proof of that ability, and as you come to understand that desire is the beginning of all creation, and as you identify, clearly, what it is that you desire, then you will continue your magnificent deliberate creating as you have begun it with your birth into this physical life.

56

As you have entered this physical life experience, you have intended a continuation of growth. You have intended interaction with others that you might learn from what you perceive, and that you might uplift others by the clear expression of your very being, others who participate with you in this physical realm, and all others who are connected and observing.

You have intended to be who you are. A perfect, ever changing, wanting, growing, magnificent being. A being who reaches out to the new, because you understand that in the new experience there is growth. You are a being filled with love, and in your purest form, you are love.

YOU ARE A BEING WHO UNDERSTOOD, AS YOU CAME INTO THIS PHYSICAL LIFE EXPRESSION, THE VALUE OF BEING AS YOU ARE AND OF ALLOWING ALL OTHER BEINGS TO BE AS THEY ARE -- for you understand that some of them are now as you once were, and others are as you will be on this continuum of evolvement.

We express our perspective of your intentions, as you have entered into this physical life experience, that we might strike some cord of remembrance within you, for as you remember the specific and deliberate and intense reasons that you have chosen this physical life experience, it will renew your zest to participate therein.

December 25, 1987

YOU ARE THE CREATOR OF YOUR PHYSICAL LIFE EXPERIENCE. We say that, because we are wanting you to understand that it is you who chooses, and, in fact, creates the life experiences, which come one at a time -- which ultimately make up, what you would term, the physical life experience.

Many of you sense that you have great purpose in being here, and as you are searching for your life's purpose, you may misunderstand, by thinking that there is a plan that has already been decided by someone else, or even by you at another time, that you must spend this life experience groping around, trying to find your life's purpose, so that you may fulfill it.

It is true, you did enter this physical life experience with some definite intentions -- BUT YOU ARE DOMINANT IN THIS TIME. THROUGH YOUR PHYSICAL CONSCIOUS THOUGHTS, YOU ARE CREATING YOUR LIFE EXPERIENCE, HERE AND NOW.

We are wanting to help you understand how those intentions that you held as you entered physical form merge, or blend, with the current creating that you are doing.

In order for you to understand that blending, you must step back a bit and try to view yourself from a broader perspective. You must see yourself as a being who has lived thousands of lifetimes, physical and nonphysical, and who has gained knowing through all of those life experiences. And as you view yourself, or attempt to, from that broader perspective, perhaps you can get a glimpse of a being who is very, very wise. A being who has been evolving through life experiences. And as you become comfortable with the existence of this broader, wiser, certainly older Inner Being -- you will have the benefit of the wisdom and knowing that it holds.

As you monitor the way that you feel as you participate in your various physical activities, the very emotion that you feel -- which is coming from your Inner Being -- will help you to know whether you are enhancing that which you have intended from your broader Inner Being, or whether you are not.

As you participate in this physical life experience, intending many things -- if you do not continue to make conscious deliberate decisions, your Inner Being, nevertheless, will guide you in the direction of those decisions that it knows that you held as you came to physical form. And that is the reason

that many of you are sensing a sort of urging from within.

What we are encouraging, as we attempt to stimulate your thoughts with our words, is a wondrous blending of your Inner Being and inner world and inner knowing with your conscious thinking physical world.

AND AS YOU ARE SENSITIVE TO YOUR EMOTIONAL STATE OF BEING -- YOU WILL HAVE SUPREME GUIDANCE FROM WITHIN.

Of course, the ultimate beneficial results will be accomplished as you are making many conscious deliberate decisions in this physical world, in which you are dominantly focused, while you monitor the effectiveness of your creation by paying attention to the way that you feel, or to the communication that comes forth from within.

And as you make more decisions about what you are wanting, your Inner Being will give you more specific guidance about whether you are on track.

9

A Time of Awakening

December 27, 1987

While, <u>individually</u>, each of you who are in physical form have the ability to create anything that you can imagine -- you enhance the experience of one another, tremendously, as you participate in this physical life together.

As you are individually making decisions and as you are individually creating, you are cooperating to enhance the creations of one another.

At times we can see that it might be an advantage if you had some time alone here in this physical life experience, for in that time you would understand, more clearly, that you are the creator of your life experience.

Without a world full of people, there would be few others to blame or to give the credit for the creating that is going on around you.

But you have not chosen a life experience alone, you have chosen a life experience where there are many. And in such a life experience there is great opportunity for satisfaction.

For the most part, those of you who are in physical form at this time upon planet earth hold an intention of uplifting others, and you receive upliftment when you are aware of the upliftment of others.

As you participate in this physical life experience, a very powerful source of satisfaction and contentment comes from your observation of the joy that is being received by others. And as you are involved with an evolving group of beings where more and more are seeking joy, then you will also be involved with a group of beings where more and more are receiving joy -- for nothing is received that is not sought -- and unless you are seeking, you certainly will not find it.

Each of you has specifically and excitedly chosen this particular time to be involved in what is taking place upon this planet, for you understood, prior to your coming to physical form, that this would, indeed, be a time when more beings would receive upliftment than any other time upon planet earth.

For the most part, man's evolvement upon planet earth has been rather gradual, and while there have been segments in history that have been speeded up, THERE HAS NEVER BEEN A PERIOD OF TIME UPON THE FACE OF THIS EARTH WHERE EVOLVEMENT HAS BEEN SO RAPID AS IT WILL BE IN THE TIME THAT IS TO COME.

December 29, 1987

You have chosen to share your physical life experience with others not because you need them to effectively create, but because participating with others enhances your experience.

EACH OF YOU, INDIVIDUALLY, HAS THE ABILITY TO CREATE ANYTHING THAT YOU CAN IMAGINE -- but as you are interacting, you benefit from the examples of one another.

You attract others, and are attracted by others, depending upon the current intentions that you hold in any point in time.

You have, undoubtedly, come into contact with others where there was immediate at-oneness experienced by both of you, and in such cases, it is very possible that you are old friends who have participated in, perhaps, many physical life experiences and have agreed, prior to this physical birth, to reunite to participate again. Many of you are finding one another now. You are coming together in this life experience because your Inner Beings have agreed that you would.

But even as you have made some decisions about others with whom you will interact in this physical lifetime, you are attracting only those beings who enhance that which you are currently thinking about.

Our point, here, is that you are dominant in this physical experience, and no matter what decisions have been made prior to this physical birth, you are attracting the others with whom you are interacting, through your physical conscious thoughts.

You have only to intend, now, in your new awareness, that you will meet those with whom you have agreed to participate -- and it will be.

This physical lifetime will be a sort of wonderful reunion for all beings who are aware of these possibilities -- for as you are aware of the broadness of your being, and of the broadness of others with whom you share this earth, and as you recognize that you emanate from groups of beings who have evolved similarly -- then you may deliberately attract those physical representatives into your physical experience that you may all benefit from the interaction.

As man has evolved, over the centuries, there has always been some recognition, by a few, of the interconnectedness of man, but in this physical life experience, many will come to understand.

THIS IS LITERALLY A TIME OF AWAKENING. A time when more of you will be aware of the true nature of your beings. And during this process of awakening, you will experience tremendous satisfaction and joy.

62

We participate with you to help you to a sooner recognition of this awakening, that you may experience more of the joy and satisfaction that is to come. For as some of you become aware and speak to others, who speak to others, there will be more opportunity for participation for more of you.

It is with great enthusiasm that we interact with you in this time. Not intending to do for you what you have intended to do for yourselves. Not intending to give information to you before you are ready to receive it, and not intending to discover for you, that which you have intended to discover on your own, BUT, WE INTERACT AS FRIENDS, FROM YOUR INNER WORLD, WHO HAVE AGREED TO PARTICIPATE WITH YOU IN THIS TIME -- THAT THERE MAY BE A BROADER PARTICIPATION IN THE AWAKENING OF MAN THAT IS OCCURRING UPON THE EARTH IN THIS TIME.

December 31, 1987

Physical man continually seeks to solve the mysteries that surround his very existence, for there is much that is not known.

But, as man explores, using the conscious physical perspective that is currently his to use, he is limited to the discovery of those things that are within that conscious physical realm. Therefore, as he searches, consciously, through physical perception, he will not discover that which he seeks, for it is not there to be found.

What is needed, for man to understand more clearly who he is, is a broader perspective. He must step outside of his conscious physical perspective in order to view that which is outside of the conscious physical realm. The simple process has been described earlier in this book, of quieting, or ignoring, conscious physical perception, that there may be a keener awareness of an inner perception.

More beings are accomplishing this quieting of the physical, and as that is accomplished and practiced -- there is a blending of the conscious physical being and the Inner Being.

Each of you, as you made your decision to be a part of this physical life, knew that this would be a time when more beings would become aware of the total nature of their being, and BECAUSE YOU WERE WANTING TO BE A PART OF THIS GRAND AWAKENING, YOU WERE EXCITED ABOUT PARTICIPATING UPON THE EARTH AT THIS TIME.

You wanted to be part of a world where more beings would know who they are and why they are participating upon the earth at this time, and to experience the blending of the conscious physical world and the broader inner world.

Your physical perception allows you a wondrous view of life experience, but as you are blending your physical perception with your inner perception, all life experience will be enhanced.

Many of you have been sensing the approaching of this time of heightened awareness. It has been written about in many different ways, by many different physical beings, throughout your recorded history.

THIS IS A TIME THAT HAS NOT ONLY BEEN ANTICIPATED BY THOSE BEINGS WHO ARE PHYSICAL UPON YOUR EARTH, BUT IT IS A TIME THAT HAS BEEN EXCITEDLY ANTICIPATED BY ALL-THAT-IS.

And from your broader nonphysical perspective, before your birth into this physical lifetime, you wanted very much to be here in your physical body to experience this wondrous time.

As beings who are wanting upliftment, not only for yourselves but for those who surround you, the potential for joyous life experience is very great in this time of heightened awareness.

As more conscious physical beings allow themselves to experience that which is beyond the physical -- THE CREATIVE VIBRATION, THAT EMPOWERS YOUR PLANET AND ALL-THAT-IS, IS INCREASING, THUS ALTERING PHYSICAL LIFE EXPERIENCE.

December 31, 1987

**We have been speaking of a time of awaken-
ing, and while you are not literally asleep, you have,
for a very long time, been suppressing an important
part of yourselves.**

In the time that is before you, many of you will awaken
that part of your awareness, to perceive from a broader perspective, and rather than seeing yourselves only as the physical conscious thinking beings that participate here upon your planet,
you will see yourselves as everlasting, evergrowing beings who
are only now, temporarily, focused in this brief, though important, encounter with physical life.

**To those of you who are sensing that there is
much more to you than you have been experiencing,
these words are reaching you deeply, for there is
great knowing within, and you are now, consciously,
harmonizing with that knowing.**

You see, in this moment, as what you are reading here is
resonating with the very nature of your being, you are accomplishing that blending between your conscious physical
thinking being and the being that is within you. And as you
trust that confirmation that comes forth from within, in the form
of emotion, you will be upon a swifter path of fulfilling the purpose that was intended as you have come to this physical form.

We hear from so many of you, "What is my purpose?
Why am I here upon planet earth?" But then you close your
eyes and ears when you are offered that which is different from
what you have heard before. You resist answers, even as you
seek.

**ONCE YOU ARE TRULY WANTING TO
KNOW, THEN THE ANSWERS COME TO YOU,
FROM EVERY DIRECTION, AND YOUR MAR-
VELOUS INNER BEING CONFIRMS.**

**Most beings, in your physical world, are not
seeking. Most have adopted beliefs that were present
around them on the day that they were born upon this
earth. And most physical beings have done no real
searching, or thinking -- on their own. And so, as**

they do not search -- it is not surprising that they do
not find.

10

The Value of Your Physical Participation with Others

January 1, 1988

THERE ARE NOT TWO BEINGS, PHYSICAL OR NOT PHYSICAL, WHO HAVE PRECISELY THE SAME PERSPECTIVE.

Those of you who are currently in physical form share many different perspectives, and those of us who are in non-physical form share many different perspectives as well.

We do not write these words in an attempt to bring you to our perspective, for we understand that that cannot be. We are not wanting to change your perspective, but to broaden it. It is our desire that you may utilize more of the perspective that is already yours by no longer suppressing the part of your perspective that is not seen or heard through your physical senses.

As you allow the blending of your conscious thinking physical being and your broader Inner Being, you will then have the advantage of ALL of the knowing that has been accumulated by you through all physical and nonphysical life experiences, instead of the limited knowing that you have accumulated only in this physical lifetime. And this blending of physical and non-physical knowing is now occurring with many of you.

You participate in your physical world with many others, for you are wanting to exercise your power of influence. Indeed, you are wanting to help others to broaden their perspective.

While your words and actions do influence, to a certain degree, your greatest power of influence comes forth as you are a blended being who speaks from the knowing that comes from within. It is not so much by your physical conscious abilities that you influence one another, but by the inner persuasion that comes forth in the form of your emotions.

You are joy seeking beings, and as you experience the knowing that comes forth from within, your joy will be multiplied many times.

You are uplifters, and while you enjoy your own upliftment, you also receive joyous pleasure from observing the upliftment of others -- and in this time of awakening, in this time when more beings will be blending their physical conscious worlds with their inner worlds, there will be great upliftment.

Each of you made the decision to be in physical form, at this time, from a part of your knowing that is not part of your conscious knowing.

You have lived many lifetimes, and from the knowing that you have accumulated through all of those life experiences, you knew the grandness of this particular physical life experience, and you eagerly made the decision to participate.

January 2, 1988

And so, we write this book from our non-physical perspective with two primary intentions: The first, to assist you in understanding the Creative Process -- that you might have deliberate control of your physical life experience, and the second, that you may come to a broader recognition of your own self -- which will enhance all parts of this physical life experience.

Our two intentions are very well blended, for recognizing communication from your Inner Being is one of the keys to effective application of the **Creative Process.**

Only when you understand and are applying the **Creative Process** to your own individual creating will you be able to effectively utilize it as you are interacting with the others who share your planet.

It is not always easy for you to understand that you are individually creating your life experience when you are involved with so many others.

As you observe others who are creating life experiences that are not in harmony with your desires, at times it seems that they are too close for comfort, and you have a feeling of fear as you are not wanting to become involved in negative situations that are happening around you. But when you understand that you will not experience that which you do not attract through the power of your thoughts, when you understand that another cannot create in your life experience -- then you will not fear the intrusion of other unharmonious beings within your life experience.

WHEN MOST BEINGS WHO ARE UPON YOUR PLANET UNDERSTAND THAT THEY HAVE THE ABILITY TO CREATE ANYTHING THAT THEY DESIRE AND THAT THEY NEED NOT BE SWEPT UP BY THE DESIRES OF OTHERS -- FOR EACH IS INDIVIDUALLY CREATING THROUGH THEIR THOUGHTS -- THEN THERE WILL BE NO MORE NEED FOR BARRICADES OR WARS OR FEAR.

You fear being swept up in negative situations that are not of your choosing, because you do not understand the Creative Process.

Everything that you experience is of your choosing, for as you give your thought and attention to a thing -- you have chosen it, for that time.

When you understand that you will not invite into your life experience that which you do not give thought to, and that the emotion that is within you will signal you about the direction of your thought, then you will know that another cannot create in your life experience, and once that is understood, your fear of what they might do in your experience is eliminated. When you understand that you have the ability to bring into your experience -- or to keep away from your experience -- anything that you choose, then you are not so threatened by what others are choosing who are around you.

As you understand that you have the power to control that which you experience, through your powerful thoughts, then you will no longer fear others, you will no longer resent others, and you will be more willing to ALLOW others to be as they are. It is important that you recognize their right to create that which they are choosing, just as you recognize your right to create what you are choosing.

If you were not living in an environment where there were many others, you would not have an opportunity to come to understand this so clearly. But as you are interacting with others, understanding and applying the **Creative Process**, you will be delighted to experience your individual freedom to create whatever it is that you are wanting, at the same time that you are allowing all others to do the same.

As you identify what it is that you do want, as you are moving through your life, one segment at a time, and as you think upon those thoughts that bring forth positive emotion -- you will not attract into your life experience those other beings who are not in harmony with your intentions. And the others who are intending, or thinking, in the directions that are not in harmony with you, will not attract you into their experience. **IT IS THROUGH THE POWER OF YOUR THOUGHTS THAT YOU ATTRACT ONE ANOTHER.**

Because most of you spend very little time identifying what it is that you do want, and because your thoughts move about from subject to subject so easily, and because you do not understand the significance of your negative emotions, you are often swept up into a negative situation, or confusion, that has been created by another. But an understanding and application of the **Creative Process** will free you from all life experience that is not precisely to your liking.

You are INDIVIDUAL creators, interacting with others that you have attracted through your thoughts, and you enter into agreements with each other in order to blend your INDIVIDUAL intentions.

It is imperative that you effectively communicate to one

another, precisely what it is that you are wanting, or expecting, from the interaction, otherwise, there is little possibility that your expectations will be met.

The beginning point of all deliberate creation is to identify what is wanted, and when you are not interacting with others, you simply make your statement of intent to yourself -- but, when there are others involved, you must communicate, clearly, with one another, what you each are wanting.

As we observe your interaction, we see that, for the most part, you do not do a good job of communicating what it is that you are wanting. You seem to assume that the others know or understand or want what you want, but without your effective and continuing communication with one another as you are making your new decisions from your ever changing vantage points, there is little possibility of continuing harmony.

Once the desire, or intention, has been identified and effectively communicated to all participants, then the **Creative Process** has begun. Once you have identified what is wanted, you have only to allow it to be, by not blocking it with negative thought, and it will be. And just as with your own individual creative endeavors, when you are interacting with others you have only to pay attention to the way that you are feeling, to know when any blocking is occurring.

An understanding of your "warning bell" Guidance System will serve you extremely well as you are interacting with others. The emotion that comes forth from within will guide you, in any moment, to help you know if you are, in that moment, creating in the direction of what you are wanting -- or if you are creating in the direction of what you are not wanting.

As you interact with another, and you find yourself filled with anger, that anger is a warning bell telling you that, in that moment, your thoughts are not in harmony with what you are wanting.

As you are interacting with another, it is most important that you communicate, segment by segment, what you each are wanting, for most of your disagreements come about, not by deliberate intent to disagree, but by default, as it is not understood, one by the other, what is really wanted.

In most cases, there is much more agreement between you than disagreement, but when you do not effectively communicate, your attention is focused upon the few areas that are NOT in harmony rather than upon the many areas that ARE in harmony.

Utilize your system for recognizing dishar-mony. In the moment that you are aware that your warning bell is ringing, ask yourself, "What thought, word or action has caused my warning bell to ring?" And then state, clearly, to yourself, what it is that you want regarding the subject. And then, most importantly, discuss it with one another.

More often than not, because you do not understand that the negative emotion is a warning bell, YOU FOCUS UPON THE NEGATIVE EMOTION ITSELF, THUS CREATING MORE OF IT, and so the anger grows, the tension grows, and THE LAW OF ATTRACTION ASSISTS BY BRINGING FORTH MORE LIKE THOUGHT, until, very quickly, you have a very large and uncomfortable argument or disagreement.

If you will recognize, at the subtle stages, that there is discomfort, and then communicate one with another -- each specifying what is wanted -- in the majority of cases, the negative emotion will not grow. It will dissipate, and in its place will be harmony and satisfaction.

Before any of this can be adequately understood it must be lived, and so, we encourage you to move forward, in the next days, utilizing the exercises that we have offered.

We encourage you to identify the segments of your day as you are moving into them, and to identify what you are wanting from each segment. And as you do that, your natural sifting process will eliminate much of the confusion that you are currently drawing into your experience, and then from your clearer, more focused perspective, you will create more of what you are wanting, and you will experience joyous harmony as you are moving through your days, one by one. As you are interacting with one another, being sensitive to the way that you

*are feeling, and communicating what you are wanting -- you will
find that all of your relationships are more satisfying.*

As you apply that which we have offered here, you will
no longer attract those beings who are not harmonious with your
basic wants, and you will interact more joyously with the beings
that you do attract. When you recognize that you, and only you,
are the creator of that which you experience, and that you may
attract, or repel, life situations by the power of your deliberate
thought, then you are freed from all fear of how someone else
might affect your life experience.

WHEN YOU RECOGNIZE THAT YOU ARE
THE CREATOR OF YOUR LIFE EXPERIENCE,
AND YOU TRUST THAT YOU HAVE THE ABILITY
TO CREATE IN THE DIRECTION THAT IS HAR-
MONIOUS TO YOUR VERY NATURE, THEN, AND
ONLY THEN, WILL YOU BE WILLING TO ALLOW
ALL OTHER BEINGS, WHO ARE UPON YOUR
PLANET, TO BE AS THEY ARE.

FROM YOUR BROADER INNER PERSPEC-
TIVE, YOU HAVE INTENDED TO BE AN AL-
LOWER, AND AS YOU PARTICIPATE IN YOUR
PHYSICAL EXPERIENCE, AND AS YOU BECOME
AN ALLOWER -- YOU WILL FIND FREEDOM.

The processes and laws that we offer are universal. They apply to all life experience, physical
and nonphysical.

Words do not teach. You gain that which you know
through real life experience, and that is the reason that you are
participating in this physical life, that you may experience that
which is new from your current perspective -- that you may acquire more knowing and another new perspective.

There is much that you already know, from the
perspective of your Inner Being, that you are not
consciously remembering, and part of the reason that
you are participating in this physical experience is
that you may bring forth part of that inner knowing
and apply it here, consciously, but you have also intended, through this physical experience that you are
now living, to evolve as a total being beyond that

which you have known before. You are wanting to understand how to create precisely what you choose, while interacting in a world where so many others are choosing so many different things. You are wanting to understand how you may participate with the others without being swept up in their creations. You are wanting to understand, clearly , that you are the sole creator of your life experience. It is wonderful that there are so many others who are willing to participate with you, for they, too, are wanting to understand how they may create independently from you.

There are sufficient numbers of others, that all thoughts may be actualized as you attract and interact with one another.

Of course, much of the creating that you do does not involve the others, but many of your creations do include others, and it is good that you are all here, together, interacting and participating in one another's creations.

IT IS MOST IMPORTANT THAT YOU UNDERSTAND THAT NO OTHER CAN CREATE WITHIN YOUR EXPERIENCE. IT IS ALL OF YOUR OWN DOING, for when you understand the Creative Process, you will enjoy the ecstasy that comes from absolute freedom.

You will come to understand, through this physical life experience, that another cannot bind you or control you or harm you or include you or influence you without your agreement. You are the sole creator of your life experience, and as you apply these processes and exercises, that are offered here, you will come to know that.

Your feeling of value will increase, tremendously, as you begin to view this physical life experience from your broader perspective.

As you recognize the value of your participation here and begin to stimulate the thinking of others because of your clear and joyous example of physical existence, not only will the beings who surround you in your physical realm benefit, but all beings will be uplifted by the knowing that you receive as you are living here.

**INSTEAD OF FEELING MORE INSIGNIFI-
CANT, AS YOU DISCOVER THE VASTNESS OF
THE UNIVERSE, YOU WILL FEEL MUCH MORE
SIGNIFICANT AS YOU UNDERSTAND THE VI-
TAL ROLE THAT YOU PLAY IN IT.** When you recognize that that which you live is being re-
ceived by many more than only you, then the value of what you
think and speak and do will be brought into proper perspective.

**You are marvelous, creating, joy seeking be-
ings -- and you have intended to experience all of
that here in this physical life.**

As you arrive, as new physical beings, you are surrounded by others who have arrived before you, and they were
surrounded by others who arrived before them, and so on.

**EACH OF YOU ARE BORN INTO A SET OF
BELIEFS THAT HAVE BEEN CREATED AND
RECREATED IN THE LIFE EXPERIENCES OF
THOSE WHO PRECEDE YOU.** The tendency is for you
to be stimulated by those beliefs and to recreate them into your
own life experience. A sort of process of absorption, it seems.
But that was not your intention from your broader perspective as
you made the decision to be a part of this physical experience.

You intended to evaluate from your ever changing perspective and to live life experience that would bring you new
knowing. You intended to assist in the evolution of the thinking
of those who are inhabiting the planet earth -- not to absorb the
thoughts that had already been thought.

**While we agree that there is more comfort in
thinking old thoughts over and over again -- we will
not agree that there is more satisfaction or more joy
or more creativity.**

As you are participating here, as a being who is seeking,
as a being who is reaching out to life experience and evaluating it
from the feeling that comes forth from within as each new experience touches you -- then you are a being who is experiencing
tremendous growth.

We interact with you, enthusiastically, in your time, for
we enjoy, very much, offering some stimulation of thought that
may very well be the catalyst for new thought and new creation

in your life experience. And although we cannot offer you a physical example -- as we participate with you through this book -- there is much value for those who are seeking.

YOU HAVE CHOSEN THIS TIME, PARTICULARLY, TO BE UPON THE EARTH BECAUSE YOU ARE AWARE OF THE POTENTIAL FOR GROWTH AND JOY THAT SURROUNDS THIS TIME.

From the broader perspective of your Inner Being, you know that growth comes from new thought and from willingness to experience new experience, and you also know that the tendency is to settle into life experience and not reach for the new.

IN CHOOSING THIS SPECIFIC TIME UPON THE EARTH, YOU KNEW THAT THERE WOULD BE DRAMATIC CHANGES, BOTH OF A PHYSICAL AND NONPHYSICAL NATURE, THAT WOULD BE CATALYSTS FOR MORE GROWTH FOR MORE OF YOU.

And while you have lived many joyous life experiences, you knew, at the time that you chose this one, that no other would surpass the value received, the joy received and the growth received from this one.

And now, as we move into the next pages of this book, we will express to you, from our perspective, what changes you will be experiencing, THAT YOU MAY PREPARE FOR THEM, PHYSICALLY AS WELL AS EMOTIONALLY.

11

Realignment of Planet Earth

January 4, 1988

Why are we interacting with you from our nonphysical dimension, in this time? What is the value of this interaction, and how will it enhance the life experience that you are living?

For many, there will be no enhancement, for they are not ready to receive the benefit of our experience. In fact, they are not ready to accept that we exist at all. But those who accept our purpose and existence, may benefit by being stimulated to see the earth from a broader perspective.

During the time that is just before you, upon your planet earth, more of you will recognize that you are more than you see in your physical bodies, and more of you, through meditation, will open a pathway between your physical dimension and the nonphysical dimension in which your Inner Being dwells. And as you accomplish this blending of your conscious being and your Inner Being, all parts of your experience will be enhanced.

Much of your conscious physical training is contrary to that which allows the blending of your being, but it is a natural process, and is known by all of you at some level of your knowing. In the time that is before you, more of you will become aware of the existence of this broader part of you, and through the power of your conscious wanting, the blending will occur.

Because of the physical changes in your environment, there will be less responding out of habit. Very few of the established patterns for your life experience will be untouched, and because of the radical difference in the way that you will experience physical life -- you will reach within to utilize the vast reservoir of inner knowing.

As you examine your changing earth through your physical perspective, or even through the perspective of those who have recorded, for your benefit, the activities of your changing earth, you are not able to stand back far enough, or long enough, to understand some of the longer "seasons."

Those of us who are not in physical form at this time, who are not limited to our memory of only one short physical lifetime, are aware of the history of your changing earth and we are aware that you are moving into an era -- a "season" -- of dramatic physical change. From your shorter, closer perspective it may be incomprehensible, but from our longer, broader perspective it is most routine. In fact, without exception, those of you who are now upon the earth were aware of the changes, both physical and nonphysical in nature, and you enthusiastically chose to participate, in physical form, during this time of change, because you were aware of the value for all who participate.

The revolving sphere upon which you live is in the process of readjustment. It is seeking balance. Gradually, over a very long period of time, it has gotten out of balance. What that means to you, in a physical sense, is that there will be a sudden and dramatic jolting as your planet realigns itself.

From our broader perspective, we can tell you that this has occurred many times in the history of the existence of the earth. In fact, on more than one occasion, a much more dramatic shifting has occurred than what is to be experienced now. This is a slight shifting which will bring about much devastation in some areas on the surface of your earth while other areas will be relatively free of destruction.

Now, the value that we offer you is this: We are providing you an opportunity for preparation of a physical and an emotional nature -- for as you are aware of what is to come into your life experience, from your broader inner perspective, you will not see it as something to worry about or to fear or to dread, but as something that has, indeed, been expected and anticipated with great enthusiasm.

At the time that you chose this physical time and place, you were very much aware of the opportunities for growth, for you understood the abilities and the potentials of your creative nature that have not been realized.

You understood, from that broader inner perspective, that in a time of change there is much reflection upon what is wanted. And when one is wanting, and allowing, there is much receiving, and when there is receiving, there is contentment. And so, if you do not compare what has been with what will be, but instead, if you anticipate your ability to joyously move forward, in all times -- then this time that is before you will, indeed, be one of joy and growth.

January 6, 1988

It is our intent, in this section of the book, to give you as much detail as we are able, as to what you will experience physically as your earth achieves this partial shifting upon its axis. We accentuate the word "partial", for it is important that you understand that the shifting that is about to occur will not mean the total destruction of your planet. Nor will it

mean the destruction of all that exists upon its surface. There will be, however, areas of great devastation, where those who are dwelling will not survive
-- while there will be other areas of comparative
safety.

All areas of your planet will experience tremors, and by
your standards of measuring earthquakes, the tremors will be
significant, but not so significant that everything, everywhere
will be destroyed. The land will not rupture everywhere.

Because of the tremors, many of the structures that are
less secure will be damaged. Large structures such as over-
passes and bridges may be affected. And certainly your transportation lines will be severed all around your earth. We cannot
speak with perfect accuracy as to the extent of the damage in every area, for there are many possibilities. The crust of your
earth has much variation in its strength, and we are not completely certain how these areas of strength and weakness will affect one another. Even in the areas of greatest destruction, there
may very well be pockets of survivors.

We encourage you to utilize the exercises that
have been offered here in this book, through meditation, to quiet your physical awarenesses, that you
may sense your inner awarenesses -- for you have
much access to guidance, from within, that will serve
you very well during this time of conscious un-
certainty.

As you are blended with your Inner Being, you will have
a very strong sensing, not only of when the time of greatest
danger is approaching, but about the safety of the area in which
you are present, as well.

When you understand, that by the power of the
Law of Creation, that you will be able to create any-
thing that you are wanting, including finding the ar-
eas of safety -- THEN YOU UNDERSTAND THAT
THE POWER IS WITHIN YOU TO BE AT THE
APPROPRIATE PLACE AT THE APPROPRIATE
TIME.

In other words, you are not needing a map that has been
offered by someone else. You may trust the inner knowing that

is within you. But many of you are not yet trusting that knowing that is coming forth. You do not trust yourselves to make the proper decisions on a physical conscious level, and even more, you do not trust yourself regarding the information from within, and for that reason we are writing these words, that we may stimulate the knowing that is already within you.

Recognize that the emotion that comes from within is a very strong guidance system, and when you are feeling extremely uncomfortable, and you cannot pinpoint a conscious reason for it, that there is a strong knowing coming forth from within.

We offer our expectation of the areas of greatest destruction, that you may make a decision, immediately, if you are living in such an area, to remove yourself from it, for once the tremors begin, there will not be time to evacuate.

Throughout the world, all areas which are near large bodies of water will receive much damage, for the water will be very high and powerful as a result of the severe jolting as your earth is shifting upon its axis.

In the United States the greatest damage caused by water will be on the east and west coasts of the continent. Because of the low elevation and the extremely high and powerful water, much of the coastline will literally be swept away, and large portions of those areas will no longer exist. It is our belief that much of the state of Florida will be swept away, or submerged, in that fashion.

The following information pertains specifically to the United States of America:

Aside from the damage that will be caused by water, there will also be much upheaval of land as the sudden jolting of your earth will cause the crust to push together and buckle in some areas, while it pulls apart in other areas. Many of the more dangerous areas have already been pinpointed by scientists who have been recording the movement of the earth's crust. A well known earthquake activity area which will receive tremendous damage runs lengthwise down the state of California affecting major populations from San Francisco, to San Diego, and even into Mexico. Another area of greater destruction, caused by earthquake and volcanic activity, will begin near the northern border of the United States, coming through the state of Idaho, through the state of Utah, through the state of Arizona and into the state of New Mexico. Another area of greater destruction will surround the area of the Great Lakes, south to the Mississippi river and to the southern boundary of the United States. The east coast will receive earthquake damage as well as the damage that will be caused by water.

Much information has already been gathered by those who have been studying the activity of your changing earth, and that information will be of value to you as you are choosing your places of safety. The areas that are near the fault lines should be avoided. Areas that are near any sign of volcanic activity, should be avoided. And areas that are near large bodies of water, even lakes, should be avoided.

You may have already recognized that there are more areas of safety than there are of devastation. And so, it is a matter of intending to be in an area of safety with a clear intent for continuation of this physical experience.

We encourage those who are intending to remain in this physical dimension to begin, at once, preparing for a time of short supply, for as your transportation lines are severed, many of the sources for food, and other things that you are wanting, will not be adequate for the numbers who are seeking.

Each of you, absolutely, have the ability to create whatever you are wanting, whenever you are wanting it, and so we agree that it is not necessary for survival, to make this preparation, but we encourage it, because as you are prepared physically, as well as emotionally, you will be in a position of strength, and more able to focus your creative ability upon the task of rebuilding and of encouraging others.

From your position of preparedness and strength you will be of much more value to those who surround you than if you are unprepared.

We offer these words to you, that you may have an opportunity to digest the information and to make a clear decision about what you want to experience during the shifting and the realignment of your earth. You have great control over the way you participate within this experience.

LIKE THE SEASONS, OR THE SETTING OF THE SUN, THE SHIFTING OF THE EARTH UPON ITS AXIS IS OUTSIDE OF YOUR CREATIVE ALTERATION -- BUT YOUR EXPERIENCE WITHIN IT IS CLEARLY NOT OUTSIDE OF YOUR CREATIVE ALTERATION.

And so, in these next months, we encourage you to think about what you want -- to remain in physical form, or not -- envisioning the life experience that you intend. Begin creating your future, now, through the power of your creative thought.

We interact with you because we have agreed that we would and because we understand your intent regarding this event. We are aware of your intentional and enthusiastic participation within this event from your broader inner perspective, AND WE OFFER THESE WORDS TO YOU, THAT YOU MAY BRING THAT KNOWING FORTH FROM YOUR INNER BEING TO YOUR CONSCIOUS AWARENESS, SO THAT THE EVENT WILL NOT BE ONE OF TRAGEDY AND UNHAPPINESS -- BUT, INSTEAD, A FULFILLMENT OF THAT WHICH HAS BEEN EXCITEDLY ANTICIPATED SINCE LONG BEFORE YOUR BIRTH INTO THIS PHYSICAL LIFE.

January 7, 1988

There is excited anticipation, from your Inner Being, regarding the events that are about to occur, for from that perspective, you are keenly aware of the value of change and of new experience.

Your Inner Being understands that change and new experience are valuable catalysts to receive growth, and growth is a primary intention for participating in this life experience. Your physical conscious inclination is to get things to a more stable point so that you will not need to experience change. You seek points of comfort, and we agree, there is not much comfort when there is continual change.

As you accomplish the blending that we have been speaking about, of your Inner Being and your conscious physical being, you will CONSCIOUSLY begin seeking experiences that will bring forth growth, for in those growth experiences will come tremendous joy and much satisfaction.

If you are looking at the dramatic changes that will take place upon your planet earth during the next years, from the perspective of one who seeks the comfort of sameness, then you will find great dissatisfaction and unpleasantness in that which is to come.

If you are viewing the events that are to come, from the perspective of one who seeks growth, and understands that growth comes from new experience, then you will be filled with excited anticipation -- for you know that within the new experience will come growth and joy.

It is our knowing, that once you have an opportunity to digest this information, that most of you will emerge with a healthy anticipation of this event, and while some of you are satisfied with the life experiences that you have created, more of you are experiencing unrest and dissatisfaction.

FOR THE MOST PART, YOU ARE NOT CONTENT AND JOYOUS BEINGS -- FOR YOU ARE NOT DOING THAT WHICH BRINGS FORTH CONTENTMENT AND JOY.

Intending, then allowing, and then receiving, is what brings forth contentment and joy. And most of you have withdrawn from the position of making decisions about what you want.

The realignment of your earth will bring more of you, simultaneously, to a point of thinking of what you are wanting.

AS YOU FOCUS UPON WHAT IS MOST IMPORTANT TO YOU, YOU WILL RECEIVE THE SATISFYING LIFE EXPERIENCE OF CREATING IT. And much of the confusion that stifles your deliberate Creative Process will be immediately eliminated, as only those things that are most important will have your attention.

It will be a time of clarity of purpose and of thought. A time of more deliberate creating. And while many of you will continue to create by default, more of you will be actively creating in the direction of that which you are intentionally thinking about, and more beings will come to understand the **Creative Process**.

A planetary shift is not needed to have this knowing, and it is not something that is being thrust upon you as a punishment, or as a cleansing. It is a physical event, brought about by the characteristics of the earth in its physical dimension, just as your seasons are. And as you know, consciously, approximately when to expect summer and winter and spring and fall -- from your broader all-knowing perspective, you are also aware of this new "season."

January 7, 1988

To assist you in your visualization of your preferred life experience, during and in the time following the shifting of the earth upon its axis, we offer the following information.

We preface this information with this statement of knowledge: The majority of your thoughts which bring forth fearful emotion have no valid basis.

Most often, when the emotion of fear is present within you, the thought that is present is pointed toward some unwanted event that you believe is lurking in your future, and once you understand that every future event is of your choosing -- for you are attracting those future events with your thoughts -- then you will recognize that the fearful emotion is coming forth to guide you away from thoughts of miscreation.

The emotions that you feel, are ALWAYS responding to the present moment. Therefore, if fear comes forth because of your thought regarding the future, recognize that there is no basis for that fear -- since you can alter the future by altering your thoughts. And recognize that as you allow fearful emotion to persist, you are also allowing creation toward that which you fear.

AND SO, WE OFFER THIS INFORMATION, NOT TO GIVE YOU SOMETHING TO FEAR, BUT SO THAT YOU MAY MAKE SPECIFIC PLANS OF PREPARATION THAT WILL ASSIST YOU IN A MORE EFFECTIVE VISUALIZATION OF A TIME OF COMFORT AND SURVIVAL.

At the time of the sudden realignment, and for many months thereafter, the entire surface of the earth will experience significant tremors. There will be a severe jolting at the beginning, and then continual, but not so significant, tremors as a sort of settling down process occurs.

In some areas, as we have noted earlier, there will be great upheaval of land, and much loss of physical life for those who are present in those areas at the time of the earth shift. But many more areas will not experience an upheaval of land, while there will be significant tremors experienced.

We encourage you not to remain inside of any building while the tremors are occurring. Your automobile will provide safer shelter.

We advise that you immediately locate an open area that is free from the possibility of something falling upon it. Avoid areas that are beneath trees, power poles or next to mountain sides or large buildings. Avoid any area where something may fall upon you.

We recommend that you put a supply of food and water and warm clothing in your automobile, so that in a moment's notice you can be outside of a building and moving quickly toward your designated place of safety. Many lives will be saved as a result of this preplanning.

Your greatest inconvenience, as a result of the impending earthquakes, will be a severe shortage of food, because your lines of supply will be severed.

We encourage you to set aside enough food and other essential supplies to last for a period of 6 to 12 months.

As you are evaluating the time and effort and dollars that are involved in that preparation, you will find that it is much less than you may think, and certainly not outside of the creative capability of anyone.

You may feel that you should make preparation for those you know who will not make preparation for themselves, and while it is a generous intention and satisfying in many ways, it is not a practical plan. As you are storing enough for yourself and for your family for 365 days, it will not be a major expense, and will not require a large amount of storage space, and you will be extremely happy that you have made that preparation.

However, if 365 of your friends, or neighbors, who have not made preparation, join you on the first day, you will all do well for that one day, but there will be much hardship as you are all met with short supply for the rest of the year.

We encourage you to be responsible for your own life experience and to encourage those who are around you to do the same. We state, very clearly, here, that you cannot create in the experience of another, nor do they want you to, from their broader, wiser inner perspective.

TRUST THAT THOSE WHO ARE WANTING WILL RECEIVE, AND DO NOT ATTEMPT TO DO THEIR CREATING FOR THEM.

In many areas, another major inconvenience will be the loss of electricity. Since much of your comfort and convenience depends upon access to electricity, we encourage you to turn your electricity off for a day or two, so that you may experience, first hand, a very clear vision of what you will be wanting. And now, while there is no short supply, you will be able to acquire that which will assist you in comfort.

There will be dramatic weather changes, all around the earth, and extremely cold temperatures even in areas that are usually warm. **Therefore, a supply of fuel and, certainly, warm clothing will be most appreciated at the time of the shift.**

There will be extreme wind and much rain in the weeks following the jolting realignment.

Volcanic ash will be experienced in all parts of your world, as the volcanos around your earth are simultaneously activated. **Face masks to protect your lungs, and goggles to protect your eyes, will be of great value.**

We are aware that you may have difficulty accepting the reality of this physical event, but we encourage you to acknowledge our broader perspective. If our words move you to no physical action, but do stimulate you to a clear, conscious, deliberate intention to continue physical life experience, we are pleased. For we understand the power of intent, and as you intend survival, and continued physical life experience, you will attract the circumstances that will provide that.

We encourage you to not only intend continuation of your physical life experience, but joyous continuation. Visualize, within your own Creative Workshop, that which you want to experience -- for as you paint the picture in your creative mind, you will be setting into motion the creation for that which you will experience.

See this as a time when the creative talents that have been, perhaps, dormant within you will surface and bring forth great satisfaction.

Imagine yourself living happily in a time of adventure, a time of change and in a time of new. SEE YOURSELVES AS PIONEERS WHO WILL EXUBERANTLY SET OUT TO CREATE, FROM A NEW PERSPECTIVE, WHATEVER SORT OF WORLD YOU PREFER.

12

A New Beginning

January 8, 1988

In the immediate time that is before you, there is potential for tremendous evolvement, for the simultaneous experience of many beings will provide a natural environment in which the Creative Process will flourish.

When you understand that magnificent creating comes through powerful wanting, through clear and deliberate thought and through high emotion, then you may understand how all of those things will be present for many beings at the same time.

Wanting, or intending, is the beginning of the Creating Process, and without it, no deliberate creation will occur.

But most of you are suppressing your desires, to avoid disappointment. When you are children, there is much that you want, but as you grow older, not understanding the **Creative Process**, you begin to suppress your wanting, to avoid the disappointment of not receiving. When you do not understand that EVERY thought creates, then you do not understand how your thoughts of doubt or disbelief push what you want away from you. And in your lack of understanding of what is keeping your wants from being realized, you gradually allow yourself to want less and less.

You have become, for the most part, people who suppress your wanting -- to protect yourselves from disappointment.

You do not remain focused upon those things that are most important, for it is difficult for you to discern which things are most important.

Because of your highly technological society, in which you have access to information from all around your earth, it is no wonder that you have a difficult time thinking about the life experience that you are living and that you are creating. Your thoughts are continually diverted, continually diffused and continually unfocused.

Because you are not focused, and because you do not allow yourselves to want, there is very little expression of positive emotion that comes forth from within.

Since there is very little of that powerful, driving, enthusiastic emotion, that is always present when you are excitedly thinking about those things that you want, it is not a wonder to us that more of you are not joyously participating in deliberate creating.

As you are reading this book, you are at the perfect point for beginning a new life experience, for as you receive that which we have offered here, your perspective will be forevermore altered.

The combination of your new understanding of the Creative Process, and your life experience during the physical changes that are about to occur upon your earth, will provide a perfect opportunity for joyous, deliberate creating, and you knew that, when you made the decision to be a part of this physical experience, prior to your physical birth into this lifetime.

It is not a creation by default that brings you to this place and time. You <u>wanted</u> to be here. You created this physical life experience, before your birth into it, by being focused with powerful, excited emotion. And so, we encourage you, now, from your physical perspective, to apply what you are reading here, and to make a decision to be clearly focused upon what you want to experience in the time that is before you. Allow yourself to feel the joyous, excited emotion of anticipation as you imagine the fulfillment of your intentions.

When you understand that you control the events of your personal experience by the power of your thought, then your focused attention to that which you want will always bring forth excited emotion -- and the excited emotion is the power that propels your creation forward.

There has never been a time, in the history of man upon this planet, that has offered the potential for more joyous creating. And since you are joy seeking beings, there is great contentment that is before you.

January 8, 1988

In this book, we have offered the key to deliberate creating within your physical life experience.

We have expressed to you the power of your thought, and we have explained that although it is difficult to control your thoughts, that it is a simple process to acknowledge the way that you feel -- and that being aware of your emotion at any point in time will guide you to a clear recognition of the direction of your thoughts and of your creating.

But, many of you believe that experiencing negative emotion means that you are weak or out of control, and so you suppress the very guidance system that will assist you in deliberate positive creation.

Some of you, rather than using the negative emotion to identify negative creativity, focus upon the negative emotion itself, and create more of it.

And others of you, identify your thought, which has caused the negative warning bell to ring, but rather than removing your attention from that thought, you continue to focus upon it, believing that until you find a solution, the negative emotion will not subside.

But your attention to the problem only enhances it and brings it right into your physical experience.

As you view the many problems from around your world, there is very little that they have to do with you, or that you can do about them. You do not feel the negative emotion because the problems exist. You feel the negative emotion about them only when you give your attention to them.

CONTINUED ATTENTION TO A PROBLEM ATTRACTS IT INTO YOUR EXPERIENCE. TO REMOVE IT FROM YOUR EXPERIENCE YOU MUST REMOVE YOUR ATTENTION FROM IT.

Many of you believe that if you give more attention to a problem you will solve it. You will find solutions, however, only as you are looking for solutions. As you focus upon the problem, your emotion will be negative, letting you know that you are creating negatively. As you focus upon the solution, your emotion will be positive, letting you know that you are creating positively.

In the time that is before you, more of you will be looking for solutions and feeling positive emotion, and much less of your attention will be focused upon the problems of the world.

January 8, 1988

Once the Creative Process is understood, you will be filled with a sense of joyous freedom, and you will no longer fear the actions of others.

No other, no matter how powerful, or how big they seem to be, has the power to create within your life experience. And if they are within your life experience it is because you have invited them through your thoughts.

YOU WILL NOT ATTRACT THAT WHICH YOU DO NOT GIVE THOUGHT TO. THEREFORE, GIVE THOUGHT ONLY TO THAT WHICH YOU

WISH TO ATTRACT -- AND GIVE NO THOUGHT TO THAT WHICH YOU DO NOT.

And once you understand that you control all that is attracted into your experience, then you will be free of fear of being violated by something out of your control. All arguments that are to the contrary, come forth from those who do not understand the **Creative Process.** Those who see themselves as victims of the actions of others do not understand the **Creative Process.** Those who blame others do not understand the **Creative Process,** for nothing comes to you without your invitation.

Recognition that you are the sole creator of that which you experience is the first step in taking deliberate control of your life.

Being in control of your life sounds wonderful to some of you, but many of you resist that thought, for you do not trust your ability. You doubt yourself.

As you recognize the broadness of your being and the vastness of your abilities and knowledge, then you will want, very much, to be the one who makes the decisions, and who thinks the thoughts that bring into your life experience that which you experience -- and you will be most unwilling to allow others to interfere in this process that you have intended for yourself.

13

Magnificent Creating in This Time of Increased Energy

January 11, 1988

From your new vantage point, the decisions that you will now make will be different from the decisions that you might have made before you read this book.

We are aware that our words have stimulated the thoughts of many of you, and for some, the knowing that is within you has come forth to confirm that which you have read here in this book, and where that has occurred you now have a totally new perspective.

And so, with your new knowing it is most important that, from the beginning of this page in this book, that you begin to make some clear and definite statements about what you currently want, for as you make those statements, through your thoughts, or as you voice them aloud, or as you write them with your pen upon your paper -- you will set into motion the creation of those desires.

IT HAS NEVER BEEN MORE IMPORTANT FOR THOSE UPON PLANET EARTH TO UNDERSTAND THE CREATIVE PROCESS, FOR NEVER

BEFORE HAS THE CREATIVE ENERGY BEEN SO POWERFUL.

Never before have your thoughts translated into actual physical manifestation so rapidly. Never before has there been so much potential for the glorious exaltation that comes with receiving that which is wanted -- and never before has there been the potential for so much painful experience from setting into motion that which is not wanted.

The time that is before you, from our vantage point, is to be a glorious time. A time of great wanting. A time of much more allowing and a time of much more receiving. And with all of that, a time of contentment, satisfaction, peace, joy, exhilaration and, indeed, ecstasy.

But each of you chooses the degree of satisfaction, contentment, peace, love, joy, or ecstasy that you will experience, for there is a broad range of that which may be experienced, and it all hinges upon your willingness to make decisions about what you want, and your belief, or knowing, that that which you think, is.

In time gone by your thoughts were not so quickly translated into their physical equivalent, but in the time that is before you, that flexibility will not be so great, and your thoughts will be translated more quickly.

Begin to practice your deliberate creating abilities, and as you recognize that you have had a thought and, in fact, have received the physical manifestation of that thought, whether it is something that you wanted or something that you did not want, stop, and say to yourself, "I have done this through the power of my thoughts and through the Laws of the Creative Process and the Laws of Attraction. This is of my doing, and it is good."

As you recognize that you are the creator of all that you experience, and as you stop trying to blame others for that which makes you unhappy -- you will be in control of your physical life experience, and you will be on your way to that exhilarating ecstasy that we have spoken of here.

As you read these words, the emotion that you feel is a very important key to help you understand whether you are creating toward ecstasy or toward unhappiness, for as you read these words, your response to them is a very strong indicator as to whether you are in harmony with the **Creative Process.**

The degree of joy or satisfaction that is felt at the receiving of something that you have created is not proportionately related to its monetary value or grandness. It is as satisfying to create a button as it is to create a castle -- if the button is something that is really wanted. **ALLOW YOURSELF TO FEEL SATISFACTION FROM EVERYTHING THAT YOU ARE INTENDING AND RECEIVING.**

We encourage you to make more decisions, in every day, about what you are wanting, and then to expect to receive those things that you have set into motion through your thought, and as you receive them, one by one, and sometimes many at one time, you will begin to realize your creative abilities.

You have come to this physical plane intending to be a magnificent creator, to transform your thoughts into physical manifestation. **IF YOU HAD NOT INTENDED PHYSICAL MANIFESTATION OF YOUR THOUGHT -- YOU WOULD HAVE REMAINED IN A NONPHYSICAL DIMENSION.** From the perspective of your broader Inner Being, you have intended to translate that which you think about into physical form, that you may understand more fully your creative power.

We offer this book with the intent of stimulating you to a clearer understanding of your abilities, and to a clearer understanding of the totalness of your being, that you may be the clear, deliberate creator that you have intended to be. The time that you have long anticipated, even before this physical birth, is just before you. We write this book to guide you from your point of inner knowing to a point of conscious recognition of that inner knowing. We are exuberant as we participate with you, as you move into this wondrous time, and we rejoice with

you each time there is a glimmer of recognition of your creative ability.

When you create, magnificently, without recognizing how you have created, we are not thrilled by your creative accomplishment. We are thrilled by your conscious recognition of the Creative Process, as you create that button, or that castle, for that is what we are here to teach.

YOU ARE TRULY UNLIMITED CREATIVE BEINGS. IN THE DAYS THAT ARE BEFORE YOU, MAKE MORE DECISIONS ABOUT WHAT YOU WANT -- AND THEN EXPECT THE PHYSICAL MANIFESTATION OF THOSE DECISIONS.

January 11, 1988

From the broader, wiser, all-knowing perspective of your Inner Being, you CHOSE to participate upon planet earth during this physical and spiritual transformation, for you understood the exhilaration and benefit that comes from new experience. You also knew that these changes are the continuation of a creation that was set into motion at the time that your earth was created, and that these physical changes would not mean the end of your planet, but a readjustment.

Your earth is seeking a balance, in this time, to assure its continuation for the physical experiences that are to come. And so, from your broader perspective, you are seeing this realignment, this readjusting of your earth upon its axis, as a "healing" sort of event -- for without it, eventually there would be total destruction of the planet.

From your conscious physical point of view, you may be resisting our knowledge about the shifting of your planet upon its axis, and you may be, very much, wanting this event not to take place. But from your broader perspective, you are not resisting it, but wanting it, for you understand the value of this realignment to the future existence of your planet, and you also understand the value of new experience that will be offered to every being who exists upon the planet at the time of the shifting, and in the time that follows.

As you are consciously physically focused, and not wanting this event, you may feel that there is a contradiction in what we are offering, for, on the one hand, we are telling you that you are an unlimited creating being, and, on the other hand, we are telling you that you cannot stop this event from occurring. And in order to understand that there is no contradiction, you must see from your inner, broader perspective, for from that point of view, you know that this realignment is part of the creation that you have set into motion from a different creative perspective, and that as you are experiencing life within this physical experience, you have accepted, and have, in fact, eagerly agreed to participate within, the changes that would occur during the realignment.

Just as you cannot gather together and intend that the sun will not rise in the morning or that winter will not come in this year, the stopping of this realignment is also outside of your creative control. However, it is most important that you recognize that your own personal experience, within that larger experience, IS within your creative control And the remainder of this book will be written in an effort to bring you to a clearer point of focusing upon what you are wanting to experience from this point forward.

The time that lies between our writing of this book and the shifting of your earth upon its axis will provide, for you, a time of adjusting and preparing, physically and emotionally, and, more importantly, will provide you a new perspective from which to make your new decisions about what you are wanting.

14

A Blending of Intentions

January 11, 1988

We encourage the gaining of your broader inner perspective, for it will afford you access to greater knowing than you have accumulated in this physical lifetime, for your Inner Being remembers all life experiences, physical and nonphysical.

This gaining of your broader perspective, or blending of your conscious thinking being with your broader Inner Being, will enhance this physical life experience, tremendously. That blending is accomplished, first, by recognizing that a broader "you" exists, next, by wanting the blending, and finally, by allowing it.

The allowing is accomplished by setting a time aside, in every day, with intent to quiet your physical conscious thinking world, that you may experience the inner world.

This process of allowing has been called "meditation," or "a quieting of the mind." It has been called many different things, and people do it for many different reasons. Some meditate to quiet the physical world, because they seek rest or freedom from physical pressures and responsibilities, while others meditate to sense their broader, more expansive, inner world.

FROM OUR PERSPECTIVE, THE MOST SIGNIFICANT INTENTION FOR THE PROCESS

OF MEDITATION IS TO FACILITATE THE OPEN-
ING OF A PATHWAY, OR CHANNEL, BETWEEN
DIMENSIONS.

ONCE A PASSAGEWAY HAS BEEN ESTAB-
LISHED, THROUGH THE PROCESS OF MEDITA-
TION, THEN COMMUNICATION CAN EASILY BE
TRANSMITTED -- AND RECEIVED -- FROM BOTH
DIMENSIONS.

From your conscious physical perspective, the advantage
in opening that pathway is that you will have greater knowing
and greater guidance from a broader vantage point.

As you open that channel between dimensions, literally
every decision that you make will be more appropriate, for your
perspective will be broader and clearer. And as you decide what
it is that you want, that decision will be transmitted through this
passageway, and will be more efficiently manifested into the
physical equivalent, or life experience.

And while all of you are now receiving communication
from your Inner Being in the form of your emotions, once your
passageway is open, the transmitting of emotion will be even
greater, and the potential for continual, harmonious, joyous creation will be greater, for you will be more aware of your Guidance System, sensing your emotions quickly, so that you may
immediately stop miscreating, and redirect your thoughts to that
which you want.

It is not our intent to distract you from your
physical life experience, for we understand your deliberate intent to be physically focused. We are encouraging a blending. An enhancement of this
physical experience that you wanted, so much, prior
to your birth within it.

For many of you, the exuberance for life, the willingness
to participate, the seeking of new experience, and the recognition
of joyous emotion, has been lost.

We are wanting to restimulate your zest for
this physical life -- and in the time that is before you,
if you are wanting it, it will be joyously re-stimu-
lated.

January 11, 1988

As you make decisions, in this day, about what you want to experience, you will set into motion the creation of that. You are the one who literally molds your future experience.

As you accomplish the blending of your Inner Being with your conscious physical being, you will gain an excited anticipation for that which is before you. And as you set thoughts of what you want into motion, in combination with the excited emotion that comes forth from your Inner Being, you will be in the perfect position to create that which you desire.

With all creation, the more specific you are about what you want, the more specifically you will receive that which you want. The more vague you are in stating what you want, the more vaguely you will receive that which you want.

There are some who believe that if they are too particular, that it will limit their chances of receiving, but they do not understand that THE CREATIVE PROCESS ALLOWS YOU TO RECEIVE ALL THAT YOU CAN IMAGINE.

We encourage you, as you anticipate your future -- your future that is one second ahead, or your future that is one year ahead -- that you be as specific and deliberate as possible. Take time, in every day, to identify your dominant intentions, for as you are living life and gaining experiences, one by one, your perspective is being altered, and as your perspective has changed, that which you want may have changed as well. Certainly, as you have read this book, your perspective has changed, and as you have an opportunity to absorb that which you have read here, and as you accomplish the blending of your Inner Being -- your perspective will again be changed.

Recognize, in every day, that your perspective has changed, and make a new statement of what is most important to you from your current perspective.

As you state an intention -- and release it to the universe, expecting the receipt of it -- it should not be necessary for you to do that again, for the Laws of the Universe, and the Creative

101

Process, in fact, ALL-THAT-IS, will go, immediately, to work upon producing, for you, the creation of that which you have set into motion. It is law. However, it is of value for you to continually reaffirm that which you are wanting, because your perspective is changing, and therefore, that which you want changes.

It is also important to continually restate your intentions, to avoid negative influence. Even though you may have intended health, and should not have to intend it again and again to continue to receive it, because of the significant stimulation toward illness that surrounds you, it is of value for you to continually counter that negative stimulation by restating your intention of perfect health.

ANY CREATION THAT YOU SET INTO MOTION, WILL BE, UNLESS YOU GIVE THOUGHT TO SOMETHING THAT COUNTERS IT.

In your multifaceted world, with your highly technological communication system, there is a tremendous amount of stimulation of thought that is received by you that is counter to that which you want. And so, conscious affirming, in every day, of what you are most wanting, is of tremendous value.

From your new vantage point that has come about because of reading this book, you will experience significant change. Most of you have not experienced much change in a very long time, and you have not received much growth. And so, as you are blending the intentions of your Inner Being with the intentions of your conscious being, the wanting for growth will draw many new experiences.

We write this segment of the book because we are wanting you to understand that you have the ability to create your experiences, in whatever way that you choose.

To say, "I want growth," is a good thing. However, to say, "I want growth through joyous experience," gives you more deliberate control. Recognizing that the earth is about to shift upon its axis, and that there will be much destruction and loss of life, your intent may be, "I want to survive this shifting of the earth upon its axis." But we are encouraging even more deliberate and specific creating. We encourage you to intend not only to survive, but to survive in joy. We encourage you to intend a wondrous life experience, even during this time of great destruction.

AS YOU WANT TO CONTINUE THIS PHYS-ICAL LIFE EXPERIENCE, YOUR CREATIVE MECHANISM, YOUR INNER BEING, THE ENTIRE UNIVERSE, LITERALLY ALL-THAT-IS, WILL AS-SIST YOU IN THE FULFILLMENT OF THAT IN-TENTION.

As you think only of surviving, never allowing thoughts of not surviving, never giving your conscious thought to that which brings forth fear or negative emotion, then you will create the experience of surviving.

As you visualize yourself safe and warm and growing and exhilarated and joyous -- then that is the life experience that you will draw.

We recognize that for many of you there will be a time of adjustment, for these words regarding your planetary disruption are not easily heard, but it is our knowing that the utilization of the exercises that have been offered here will lead you to a clear understanding of the very principles of life that you are wanting to understand.

An application of the principles that you have read, here in this book, and the experience of your earth shifting upon its axis, are a wonderful combi-nation. You anticipated that it would be a good time to be here, and, indeed, you were right.

15

Applying the Creative Process for Harmonious Interaction in This New Age

January 11, 1988

THE TIME THAT IS BEFORE YOU, IN THIS PHYSICAL LIFE EXPERIENCE, PROMISES TO BE A TIME OF GREAT SATISFACTION AND PEACEFULNESS AND CONTENTED JOY, FOR IT IS A TIME WHEN MORE OF YOU -- AS YOU ARE UNDERSTANDING THE CREATIVE PROCESS, AND ARE APPLYING IT -- WILL RECOGNIZE THAT YOU HAVE ABSOLUTE FREEDOM.

As you understand that another cannot create in your life experience, and, that another will not be a part of your life experience unless you invite them -- through your thoughts -- then you are truly free. You are not wanting to be free of experience with other beings, for if you had wanted that, you would not have chosen a physical experience where you are surrounded by others.

YOUR INTERACTION, ONE WITH AN-OTHER, ENHANCES YOUR LIFE EXPERIENCE.

You will find that through the power of your thought, and through the power of your intentions, you will draw those beings to you who are harmonious, in intent, with you. And you will repel those beings who are not in harmony with your intentions.

If your intentions are not clear, then you will attract confusion, but as you are more specifically defining, in every day, what you want, then you will, more specifically, draw those individuals to you who will enhance that.

And as you attract those of like intent, you will have joyous interaction. And as you recognize that the others who are of different intent need not influence your life experience or be attracted into it -- then you will no longer feel that you need armies to protect yourselves, or barricades to keep others away from you. Then you will understand that by the power of your thought you will not invite them into your experience.

And once you understand the power of thought, you will joyously experience your own freedom to express and to be as you are -- while you will be willing to allow all others the same freedom. As more of you reach this state of being, it will be a time of peace and a time of contentment and a time of wondrous joy upon your planet earth.

Now this all sounds very wonderful, but how do you take the words that you have read here and begin to apply them to your own physical life experience?

The Law of Attraction and the Law of Creation are universal. They apply to all dimensions and to all experience, physical and nonphysical. And just as they apply to your individual creating, to that creating which does not involve others, such as the maintenance of perfect health -- they also apply to that which you create, through the form of your agreements, one with another.

To have a wonderful relationship with another physical being must be wanted by both beings, or it will not be. Since you cannot create in the life experience of another, each of you must want, and therefore set forth, the creation of this fulfilling relationship. And whether it is a personal relationship or a relationship of business, the intentions of each being involved enter into the satisfactory culmination of that relationship.

Once a relationship has been established, as with any creation, the desire for continuation must be there, or the relationship will not continue. ALL

CREATIONS ARE THE SAME. ONCE YOU HAVE CREATED A THING, IN ORDER TO MAINTAIN IT, OR TO CONTINUE IT, YOU MUST CONTINUE TO WANT IT -- OR GIVE ATTENTION TO IT -- OTHERWISE IT WILL DRIFT OUT OF YOUR EXPERIENCE.

As you understand and apply the Creative Process, as you are individually creating, and as you become more sensitive to the "warning bells," that you may stop your miscreating in the moment that it begins -- then you may apply that knowing to harmonious creating with others through your agreements with them.

When a negative emotion is present within you, and you recognize that your frustration, or anger, is your warning bell, signalling to let you know that, in that moment, your thoughts or words or actions are not in harmony with your agreement, you must stop, immediately, and remind yourself what it is that you are wanting, for as you allow the anger, or frustration, to remain, you are also allowing miscreating. And since this creation not only involves you, but the others with whom you have entered into the agreement -- it is most important that you communicate, one to another, what it is that you each are wanting.

As each of you focus upon that which you want, upon the agreement between you, the emotion of anger, or frustration, will subside, and so will the negative creating. AND AS YOU FOCUS UPON WHAT IT IS THAT YOU ARE WANTING -- YOU WILL BEGIN CREATING IN THE DIRECTION OF THAT WHICH YOU WANT.

More of your agreements are not satisfactory, and more of your relationships do not remain intact, because most of you do not yet understand the Creative Process.

Most of you believe that before a negative emotion will go away that you must fix what you believe has caused it. You feel that you must think about the problem, and stew over the problem, until you finally are able to remove the problem, and then once the problem is removed, the negative emotion will go away. But that is not the case.

AS LONG AS YOU REMAIN FOCUSED UPON THAT WHICH HAS BROUGHT FORTH NEGATIVE EMOTION, YOU WILL CREATE MORE OF IT.

January 12, 1988

An understanding and application of the Law of Attraction and the Law of Creation, will bring about many changes in your life experience.

You will find a new stream of people flowing into your life experience while many of those who were already a part of your experience will drift away, for as you begin to clarify that which is important to you, you will begin to attract those who are wanting more of the same things that you are wanting, while you release those who are not, and in the process, you will experience less conflict, less confrontation and less negative emotion.

And now, from your new perspective, as you begin to understand and apply the **Creative Process** -- with those beings that you are attracting who are of similar intent -- you will begin a glorious new life experience.

And once you understand, and are applying the Creative Process in that which you create apart from any other individual, then you will be able to understand how it applies in your creating as you participate with others.

BRIEF REVIEW OF THE CREATIVE PROCESS

Make more decisions, in every day, of what you intend, and as you do that, know that you have become an automatic sifter who will attract those beings and circumstances that will enhance that which you want, while you will ignore, or repel, those beings or circumstances that do not enhance that which you want.

Understand that all thought that you give toward that which you want furthers the creation of it, and that positive emotion speeds the creation. And as you are moving through your day, be sensitive to the way that you feel, and recognize those negative warning bells at their early subtle stages. Then bring to your conscious mind the thought or word or action that has caused the warning bell to ring, and replace that thought with a thought of what you do want, and feel the negative emotion transformed to positive emotion.

Now, as you are interacting with others, the same process may be applied.

As you are interacting with others, in personal, social or work relationships, **IT IS MOST IMPORTANT THAT EACH OF YOU, INDIVIDUALLY, IDENTIFY WHAT IT IS THAT YOU WANT FROM THAT RELATIONSHIP, OR AGREEMENT OR PARTICIPATION, AND ONCE YOU HAVE DECIDED, IT IS MOST IMPORTANT THAT YOU COMMUNICATE IT TO ALL OTHERS WHO ARE INVOLVED WITHIN THE AGREEMENT.**

You see, most agreements are unsuccessful because of the lack of clear communication. It is as if you expect one another to know what you know or to be who you are -- but another can not see from your perspective, and you must use your power of words to bring them to an understanding of what you want.

Not only is it important that you begin your agreements with clear communication, with each stating what is wanted, but it is important that this be a continuing dialogue, FOR YOU ARE ALL CHANGING BEINGS, AND FROM DAY TO DAY -- EVEN FROM MOMENT TO MOMENT -- THAT WHICH YOU EACH WANT MAY CHANGE.

In those relationships or agreements that are most important to you, it is of value to have a brief session in every day to restate what you each want, FOR NO CREATION IS EVER COMPLETED. Your creations are moldable and pliable, they are not made of concrete, and that is good, for you are a changing being. Therefore, what you are wanting is a changing thing, and as you apply your new thought, from your new perspective, you literally alter the creation of those things that you want.

Communication is important because you are not changing equally, but you usually have far more things that are in harmony with those you interact with, than things that are not in harmony.

As you sit together, intending to speak about that which you harmoniously want, your attention will be drawn to that which you do want, and away from that which you do not want. You see, your disagreements come about as one or the other, or perhaps all, are focusing upon that which you do not want.

THERE ARE NOT TWO OF YOU WHO ARE IDENTICAL, AND EVEN IF YOU WERE IN ONE MOMENT, IT IS NOT LIKELY THAT YOU WOULD BE IN THE NEXT, FOR YOU ARE ALL CHANGING BEINGS.

And so, the key to harmonious relationships is not that you find others who are exactly like you, but that you focus your attention upon your points of harmony, FOR THE NEGATIVE EMOTION COMES FORTH ONLY WHEN YOU THINK OF THAT WHICH YOU DO NOT WANT.

Even as an entire body of people upon your earth, you have more points of harmony than you do disharmony. The basic nature of your beings is much more harmonious than it is unharmonious. BUT YOUR WARS AND YOUR DISAGREEMENTS COME ABOUT BECAUSE YOU DO NOT LOOK AT THOSE THINGS THAT ARE HARMONIOUS, YOU LOOK AT THE THINGS THAT ARE NOT. And since you are not able to change those things, for you cannot create in the life experience of another, you cause yourself great distress, and you bring much negative experience into your life as you give your attention to those things that cause you negative emotion.

As you understand that your primary intentions are harmony and growth and that the primary intentions of those who surround you are the same, and as you recognize that even in your differences you are each intending to have life experience that will bring you knowing, THEN, PERHAPS, YOU WILL BE

MORE WILLING TO ALLOW THE OTHERS TO BE AS THEY ARE, AS YOU EXPECT THEM TO ALLOW YOU TO BE AS YOU ARE. And as more of you are reaching that state, then there will be total harmony upon your planet earth, and peace and satisfaction and contentment and joy.

As we speak of the total world, it is difficult for you to find your place within it, so, instead, let us talk of those individual experiences in which YOU participate.

When you understand and trust the **Law of Attraction**, and when you are effectively making strong, clear statements of what you want, you will find yourself surrounded by those beings who enhance that wanting.

If you will trust that you will experience only that which enhances what you want, then you will not be so likely to look for flaws within those individuals that surround you. Then you will expect the relationship to be one of enhancement, and you will allow it to be that way.

You live in a society where much criticism abounds. Through your television and radio and newspapers there is much more searching for disharmony than there is searching for harmony. There is much more criticism than praise. But you need not participate within that attitude, and, in fact, you must not, because you are seeking harmony. The negative emotion that you feel as you listen to those broadcasts, or even as you listen to the negativity of a friend, is a very powerful signal to you from your Inner Being letting you know that, in that moment, you are miscreating.

As you learn to move through your day, seeking joyous emotion, and you begin to recognize, at the early stages, whenever you are experiencing a negative emotion, and then you deliberately change your thought, which will change the emotion -- you will then be upon the path of continuous deliberate creation. And that is the purpose of this book. To guide you to that point of understanding and to that point of being.

It may seem to be an oversimplification of life, to you, as you read these simple laws, but as you begin to apply them to every life experience in which you participate, and as you see the complexities of life that have troubled you become clear, and as you see your desires become manifest into physical experience, and as you see yourself surrounded with those beings who are wanting harmony and growth as you do -- and as you are feeling exhilaration of accomplishment, you will truly know the value of understanding and deliberately applying these laws to each of your life experiences.

January 12, 1988

Since wanting is the beginning point of all creation -- it is of great advantage for you to spend time, in every day, evaluating what it is that you are wanting, from your CURRENT perspective.

In light of the information that you have received, here in this book, this is a perfect opportunity to visualize your world exactly as you would like it to be, because in the time that is just before you, you will be at a new beginning point in many areas of your life.

And many of your old habits and much of the influence of others, that now hinder you, will no longer exist, and your vantage point will be fresh. You will be closer to a purer state of wanting than you have ever been in this physical experience.

If you will look upon the time that is to come as a refreshing new beginning whereby you will utilize your own creative ability, then you will find yourself filled with excited anticipatory emotion rather than the emotion of dread or fear.

As you set forth, through the power of your thought, a picture of that which you would like to experience, you will begin attracting others who are in harmony with those thoughts. You all create from your current perspective, and ordinarily that perspective changes very slowly. But the events that are about to take place upon your planet will, literally, jolt you into a new perspective, and many of the beliefs, and many of the habits, that have bound you to old perspectives will no longer exist in your experience.

We encourage you to begin, now, envisioning your life experience as you would like it to be, and we encourage you to be sensitive to the way that you feel as you set these thoughts into motion, seeking always that positive emotion that indicates deliberate and positive creation.

The **Law of Attraction** will assist you, for as you think of that which you want, other thoughts will be attracted until you have completed the picture. And since your actions always follow the path of your dominant intentions, you will find yourself very busily readying yourself for the exciting time that is before you.

If you find that you are not moved to action, if you find yourself running in circles, not knowing what to do, then you have not yet formed your picture of what you want, for when your image of what you want is clear, then the action which will enhance that always comes very easily.

But when you are not able to move yourself to action, it is because you have not clearly defined what you want, and you have not made a decision to have it.

There are not two of you who are now physical that are the same, and there is much variation in your differences. Your intentions range from one extreme to the other. And so, there are those who are participating here in this life experience with you whose intentions are actually in opposition with yours, at this current time. As you are receiving the words that are written here, and wanting to express them to others, it is important that you understand that some of them will be receptive to these words, and others will not.

As teachers, we have learned that our work is not to convince anyone of anything, but to offer that which we know, through the power of our words, and by being who we are, and through the clarity of our being, we will stimulate the thoughts of those who are wanting something similar.

DO NOT ASSUME THE RESPONSIBILITY OF CONVINCING ANYONE OF ANYTHING. INSTEAD, MAKE YOUR DECISIONS ABOUT WHAT YOU WANT, AND SET OUT TO CREATE THE LIFE EXPERIENCE THAT YOU CHOOSE -- AND ALLOW ALL OTHERS TO DO THE SAME.

You may meet with opposition as you express to others your intentions for preparation for the shifting of your earth upon its axis. Some may consider you foolhardy, and may want to influence you in a direction that is not in harmony with your decision to be prepared, but you must resist that influence by turning your attention to that which you want.

Each of us have intended, through our life experiences, physical and nonphysical, to gain a clearer perspective of who we are and to express it, and, perhaps, influence others through the power of our example.

BUT WE MUST BE WILLING TO ALLOW EVERY OTHER BEING THE FREEDOM TO THINK AND CREATE AND BE AS THEY CHOOSE THROUGH THE POWER OF THEIR THOUGHTS. As we understand that it is not a personal affront, when another does not agree with us, but that it is their expression of their own life, then perhaps we can more easily allow the difference.

See yourselves, not overwhelmed by the decisions that are before you, but exhilarated by their potential for satisfaction and contentment. Begin now by making more decisions, in every day, about what you want, and enjoy the exhilaration that comes as you allow those decisions to manifest into physical creation.

We encourage you to begin acknowledging your ability to create, now, before the physical disruption of your planet, so that you will be prepared to apply these well developed abilities to deliberately create that which is important to you.

We offer this book to you, feeling tremendous, excited, joyous emotion, for this is the physical manifestation of our clear and deliberate intent.

As we dictate these words, we visualize them printed and bound and in your hands as a physical book. We see you reading this book, receiving stimulation of thought and a broader, clearer perspective. We see your physical life gloriously enhanced as you achieve a blending of your conscious physical being and your broader Inner Being. We see you reading with the emotion that comes forth from within, and we see you consciously deciding to continue this joyous physical experience in which you are participating. We see you making decisions that will enhance your life experience, and we see you filled with thrill bumps, again and again, as you read through the pages of this book, as the confirming emotion comes forth from your Inner Being, letting you know that you are in harmony with these words.

And finally, we visualize you making a decision to joyously and excitedly move forward in this time of change, anticipating tremendous growth for yourself, and excited about all that will be experienced by those who surround you.

As we set this creation into motion through the power of our clear and deliberate intent, we have great expectancy for the receiving of that which we desire.

Part II

Afterword

Esther has stated to me, repeatedly, that she believes that the "Abraham experience" has come about because of my intense and continuing wanting to understand. And while Esther is also wanting to understand, she is the first to admit that she seeks joyful experiences first, and learning experiences last.

It is my belief that it is the combination of our joyous life and love together that has brought to us this glorious experience of Abraham, for we are a couple blended in love, blended in joy and blended with an intense wanting to know.

And there is not much point in trying to decide why any of us are at the point we are at. Each of us are where we are, and are having the experience that we are having, because of thoughts that have been set forth before this time.

You and I are open to new learning. That is why we are, at this moment, involved in this book -- we are wanting to know more -- and because of our wanting, Abraham has written this book.

It has been more than 20 years since I first became aware that I could have anything that I truly wanted, and what I have truly wanted, has been to understand how to use my freedom to be, to learn and to change; and of major importance has been my desire to learn how to consciously get in line with the "power of the universe" so that I could flow in harmony with it -- and so that I could teach others what I was learning.

For as long as I can remember, I have expected to find answers to my steady steam of questions, and the answers have come...and the search has continued.

I was born in the "Garden of Eden," San Diego, California, and as I was learning to read, it was books that included "Aesops Fables," "the Bible" and "Bullfinches Mythology," that stimulated my interest in finding answers.

From San Diego, we moved to a series of small family farms in northwest Arkansas, where my search turned to the teachings of a wide variety of religious denominations. My parents allowed me the religion of my choice -- and I studied all that were available in those small Ozark communities. Sitting on logs in tents, benches in churches and in pews in sanctuaries, listening to beliefs that were in conflict and beliefs that were in harmony -- my search continued.

Those pre-teen years were years of extremes: illness, poverty, hard work, fear, confusion -- and continued searching -- but also, times of intense desire. And my specific desire for confidence and for a strong healthy body, brought to me the experience of performing as an aerialist, for two adventurous seasons, with a circus in Cuba -- and I was making life work for me.

Almost 30 years ago, and soon after I had ended a stint as an actor on a television series that was being filmed in Arizona, that period of experimenting, experiencing, evaluating and making life work, climaxed. I abruptly realized that life was not "working" the way I was trying to make it be -- and so the deliberate search for knowing began again.

Again, I experienced a period of investigating religious philosophies, listening, reading, questioning...in the churches, cathedrals, temples, synagogues...wherever people gathered to worship -- and as my search for understanding intensified, so did my new experiences for learning.

Some of the most wonderful experiences of my life have evolved from something that I had said "no" to before I fully understood it, and my first encounter with a Ouija board was a good example of that...Some friends, in Spokane, Washington, that I stopped to say "Hello" to, on my way to Canada, asked me to have a look at their new game. The game was a Ouija board, and I forcefully said "no" to having anything to do with it -- but my friends persuaded, and that dramatic "chance" experience opened the doors into a different dimension of exploration, and I was directed to reading books again. And so, my new mentors became Albert Schweitzer, William James, Carl Jung, Eric Fromm, Kahil Gibran, Mark Twain, David Seabury, Thoreau, Emerson, Eddy, Fillmore, Holmes...and they all, in turn, guided me to a point of concentration around Napoleon Hill's classic book, "<u>Think</u> <u>and</u> <u>Grow</u> <u>Rich</u>" -- a point that marked the beginning of another major segment of my life.

And then, twenty years ago, while enthusiastically putting into practice the principles that I had learned from Hill's book, I was doing something that I had wanted to do since my childhood, I was an operator and co-owner of a motel near El Paso, Texas. Within two years, that experience had served its purpose, and I returned to California, excited about applying my new knowing to a business relationship with a broader range of people.

And so, another exciting, new adventure was soon underway, and by the year of 1978, two years before Esther and I were married, I was experiencing the most personally and financially fulfilling period of my lifetime, up to that point. Operating from my home in central California, applying and teaching what I had learned, I was in the eighth year of the building of a multi-national distributorship, an experience that was answering nearly every want that I had ever had -- and now, a new set of questions was beginning to form, questions as to how I could, more effectively, reach and teach more people the principles that I had been learning and applying, that were serving me so well.

Esther and I met through our association in business, and on the night that we first met, it felt as though we had been best friends forever, and four years of a successful business relationship followed.

We were married in 1980, and moved to Arizona for a new beginning, but we were rarely there that first year. We toured the northwestern states with our motorhome, took repeated trips and cruises to the Virgin, Caribbean, and Hawaiian Islands -- and all the while, we continued to add to our business.

From our first moment together, twelve years ago, Esther and I have been on the same "wavelength." Abraham has told us that we have even shared the same body in other lifetimes -- a concept that is not easy to understand. For nearly every day, for over seven years, we have been together for 24 hours a day. It has been truly wonderful.

The only thing that was ever a conflict was when I would want to speak with anyone about my past Ouija board experiences with other-dimensional beings. She would even walk out of the room if I brought it up.

Esther was born into a culture, in a small mountain town, where it was taught that any conscious contact between a common earth person and a nonphysical being was "evil." It was forbidden by their rules. And so, to prevent disturbing Esther, I stopped discussing the subject at all. It wasn't something that I understood, anyway.

I had experienced about a year of the board, using a friend that it worked for (it wouldn't work for me) in order to contact many different nonphysical personalities, and nearly all of them were frivolous, fun loving, and excited about communicating with us for hundreds of hours. They were clear, concise, and entertaining -- but, they had nothing to say that was of value to me. I am entertained mostly by learning something, and their games were no more than games to me -- and so, I put an end to it.

However, I continued to cherish and to speak of those experiences, because I did come away from them with the knowing that there truly were living, willing, communicative nonphysical beings, with degrees of intelligence that seemed to rank as low as the lowest of us in physical form, but, also, higher than the highest of us. I came to the conclusion that there was a broader source of knowing available to us -- whenever we wanted to tap into it.

And so, although I knew that I would, in time, receive the answers to finding the means to receiving everything that I would ever want -- there was never an indication that this knowledge would be coming to me through a group of other-dimensional beings -- speaking and writing through my wife!

Early in 1985, a couple, in business with us, offered a cassette tape, saying that it was a "channeled" tape. We had never heard the term "channeled" used that way, but when they described the process, we recognized it as being similar to what we had been reading about in the "Seth" books. Jane Roberts, a writer, would go into a trance-like state, and a nonphysical being, who called "himself" Seth, spoke through her, dictating several extraordinary books, while her husband Robert Butts, put the words onto paper.

"Seth Speaks", a book that I had discovered while browsing in a Phoenix library, in 1983, was the first book to have any major meaning for me since I discovered "Think and Grow Rich," in 1965.

Our business partners were now telling us that the lady who had made the "channeled" tape was named Sheila, and that an entity who called itself Theo, spoke through her, and that for about the price of a consultation with our attorney, we could have a half of an hour of private time to ask any questions that we had. Well, I was excited! What a thrill; I was going to get answers to questions that I had been asking since I was six years old...

At our first 30 minute session with Theo, Esther was quiet, but I had a long list of questions that I asked. We left that session in a state of...I don't have a word for it...It was a blend of love, joy and assuredness. And Esther, her fear now replaced by love, was asking to return on the next day, because she was now ready to ask some questions.

During our session on the following day, Theo suggested, at our request for a means to advance more effectively, that Esther and I begin, together, a simple, daily mediation. They told us that we both were "channels" and that the name of our "guide" would be given to us at a later time, through a "clairaudient experience."

We returned home, changed, immediately, to comfortable clothing, set our timer to ring in 15 minutes, and then sat and focused on our breathing -- following Theo's instructions precisely -- and within a short while, something began "breathing" Esther; it was awesome and exciting, all at once. Truly a spectacular experience.

Nine more months passed, during which we quieted our minds for 15 minutes daily, but there was no repeat of that first phenomenon. There was a pleasant numbness -- but no more motion -- and then, in November of 1985, they began maneuvering Esther's head, and she became aware that they were spelling words in the air, using her nose as a pointer..."I AM ABRAHAM...I LOVE YOU...I AM HERE TO HELP YOU....January of 1986, they began to type their words...and the speaking, through Esther, began while we were driving down a Phoenix freeway, boxed in by two large trucks, and their first words were: "This freeway is too dangerous...Take the next exit."

They began their first book in May of that year. There followed, large seminars, small workshops, private consultations and radio and television talk shows -- and what a thrill it has been for me to be a part of it. It is a pleasure to see others asking and learning, as Esther and I have, and to see the joy that so many are receiving as they are having new life experiences and new growth.

Esther and I enjoy one another, and we both enjoy new experiences, new friends and new learning, and we are each excited about our part in this growing phenomenon of Abraham that we have shared these past two years.

Abraham gives us no mystical, magical help. Everything that they give us is something that we can give to the next person.

Esther and I are at one with the wisdom that Abraham has so willingly given, in response to our asking. We eagerly apply what we are learning as we enthusiastically move forward into our new life experiences -- and we are equally eager in our wanting to share the words of Abraham with you, because we are aware of the value that they can be to you -- and through you.

From the beginning, it has been our choice as to whether

to keep the words of Abraham for our personal use -- or to publish them for the use of others. The material regarding the shift in the crust of the earth came to us in their first typewritten messages, and to me, that part seemed almost out of context with our major work together, and although we have now prepared for it, physically and emotionally, we still cannot know that it is to be, until it has been, and so we have not found comfort in relating that part of the message.

However, we prefer to have prepared for the shift and it then not happen -- than to have not prepared for it, and then have to experience it, caught by surprise. And we can only assume that there are many others who would like to be aware of those same choices.

I recall the stories of the pioneers who loaded their wagons with their families and limited provisions, and by their choice -- they traveled into the unknown West for a new beginning that would be under their control. There were no jobs waiting for them, there were no houses or grocery stores or even cleared land -- there was only the freedom, and the promise, of a new beginning. They believed in their personal ability to succeed at creating a world that they had but dreamed of.

And so, as I consider your dreams, your wanting, your strengths, and your ability to decide for yourself, and as I acknowledge your power to create, for yourself -- whatever is important to you -- I then become more comfortable in your hearing what I have been hearing about the earth changes.

In the remaining pages of this book, you will find a written transcription of several group sessions with Abraham. It was difficult for us to select the sessions which were most appropriate because at the ending of every session many of those who attend regularly always exclaim, "This was the best session ever!" We have included these transcriptions, that you might see, first hand, how an understanding of the principles that you have read in the first 15 chapters of this book may be applied to day to day living.

Perhaps some of the questions that you have will be answered here in these pages. However, we are wanting you to understand that Abraham has a way of sensing even the unasked

Questions and Answers
from Group Sessions

January 20, 1988

ABRAHAM: We are extremely pleased that you are here.

As we are beginning, if you will bring to your conscious mind, as specifically as you are able, that which you are most wanting to understand, it will be of great value to you. (20 second pause.)

It is a good idea, always, when you are moving into any new SEGMENT of your life experience, and there are many in every day, are there not...that you take a moment to identify what it is that YOU are wanting, for as you do that, you become the SELECTIVE SIFTER and, in fact, DELIBERATE CREATOR of this segment.

If you do not take the time to identify what you are wanting, then you are not as deliberate, and you may easily be INFLUENCED by what is happening around you -- or by your own old HABITS that no longer apply.

As we were beginning, here, Esther stated her intent to speak clearly the words that we are offering to you. And we will state our intent to you, which is that you will be stimulated to thought.

There is really not a specific direction that we are trying to lead you. It is not that we are believing that you believe something that you should not and that we are wanting to take your focus from that and put it somewhere else. That is not what we are about.

We are teachers, and we are here to teach you the universal laws that apply to all life experience -- physical or nonphysical -- that you may enhance this physical life experience in which you are participating. And what you are wanting, regardless of what it is, is good, for it is that which you are wanting to create.

And so, what you will hear from Abraham, as you understand it and apply it, will enhance this marvelous physical experience in which you are living, for it will give you the freedom, or the control, that you know is yours -- at least from your broader perspective, you know it is yours.

QUESTION: How do we become blended to the point where we're working both ways? Both physically and nonphysically?

ABRAHAM: Without recognizing that the Inner Being exists, and without accomplishing what we are calling the blending -- which we will speak of more clearly before we are finished here -- a physical being could magnificently create, simply by focusing upon what is wanted, simply by applying what you are terming "positive thought," never giving thought to anything that is negative -- and they would create magnificently.

What we are speaking of, here, is perfect and deliberate creating. What we are offering you is absolute freedom. You see, just as important as understanding the Creative Process -- so that you may create those things that you want -- it is important that you understand it, so that you STOP creating those things that you do NOT want.

Most beings have those little things (that they do not want) that are happening in their life experience, and they don't understand it. A person who understands that if they focus upon their business objectives, and if they associate with those who are "positive thinking," upward moving beings, and they find themselves creating magnificently in the business world, may, at the same time, find themselves in the possession of cancer, or some deadly disease, because they do not understand that *all* of their thoughts create and because they have some fear that has been stimulated by some member of their family, when they were very young, and they have carried it with them, and so, all of their life, every time the word "cancer" comes up, they think about it in a fearful way, dreading it, worrying about it, hearing all of the advertisements from the television, you see.

And so, what we are offering is not just a way to help you get your car, or your dollars. What we are offering you is a way to be in complete control of your life experience, so that you may deliberately create *all* parts of it, so that you may actually attract those drivers upon the freeway, that are *also* intending safety, that you may repel those that are confused, or who are intending other than safety. Do you see?

QUESTION: OK THEN, HOW DOES ACTION GET IN THIS? If we say, "OK I want this, and it will be," and (I) don't do anything about it?

ABRAHAM: When you are wanting something, really wanting it, and you have released it to the universe, once you are blended, as we have discussed, you will receive promptings, opportunities, and you will take action. *Your ACTION follows your dominant intentions, always.* Hear that.

You are always doing something, and if you haven't identified your dominant intention, then your action and your words are following your habit or your influence from others. That is why there is so much miscreating. When you really want something, you find an easy alignment of thought, word, and action -- and that is the key. (To Questioner) Think about it, for as you think about it, there is something more for you.

There are those who would say, "Abraham, you can't really mean that all we have to do is think something into reality?"

What we are saying is that as you set your thought into

motion, not only you, but everyone who will enhance that cre-
ation will be moved to the ACTION that will bring you what you
want.

JERRY: It 's like planting an acorn in the ground. You can't
think it into a tree. Once you plant it in the ground, then the
Life Force takes over...

ABRAHAM: That is correct. That is a good story.

JERRY: Now...you said earlier, "Everything that you want is
yours." Now, I know it can, because I make sure that what I
want, I can get, first, but what if I wanted the same thing that
she wanted, and we both want it, and there is only one of them,
and so...?

ABRAHAM: Create another one.

JERRY: If I get it, she doesn't, and if she gets it, I don't?

ABRAHAM: There is not only one of anything. (pause)
YOU ARE CREATOR. You are not a gleaner or a gatherer or a
getter...

JERRY: I'm looking for answers.

ABRAHAM: You are not looking for a prize that has been
created by someone else. You are creator of the prize, and she is
creator of her prize. If you want it, create it. (To her: If *you*
want it, create it.) And both of you leave what she has created
alone. It is hers. (laughter)

JERRY: OK. How about if it's that physical cup right there?
(on table)

ABRAHAM: (pause) If you are wanting a cup, create it.

JERRY: OK

ABRAHAM: Say, every morning, when you get up, "I am wanting a cup. I am wanting it to be that color and that size, and I want those words to be written upon it." (logo)

We are upon a very important point here...It is the first time that it has been spoken, are you aware? You are the creator of *all* things. You believe that you are here in this physical world and that everything that will ever be created, is already here, and you are here fighting over it.

JERRY: Um hum.

ABRAHAM: It is the reason that you have your wars, and your walls. It is because you think there is only this much wealth, or value. And so, there is this power struggle to get enough of it in *your* corner because you do not understand that YOU ARE THE CREATOR and that the universe provides for you, whatever it is that you want, if you will allow it to be. And what you are speaking about is the blocking of the allowing. Your belief that there is only one such a cup, and that it is really hers, and that she wants it more, will keep you from ever having it...

JERRY: "I wouldn't want to take something that was that important to her."

ABRAHAM: Create your own. Understand that there is nothing that belongs to anyone. You cannot take what is hers, away. Create your own. (pause) She may give it to you, but it will not satisfy you, because you are only satisfied by what *you* create!

QUESTION: I have a question that relates to "channeling." In some instances, I've read of concerns for "channels," of "disembodied evil spirits" having access to the physical being. Can you address that?

ABRAHAM: It is a good topic, for just as you are varied in your intentions here in your physical experience, there are varied intentions in *all* dimensions.

There is not a source of "evil." In other words, as you think of your GOD as the source of "goodness", there is not a devil, or a demon, who represents the source of "evil."

The GOD FORCE, the ENERGY FORCE, that empowers ALL-THAT-IS, is consistent -- but the variance between one extreme and the other, just like the difference between hot and cold -- is the INTENT. Therefore, there *are* those whose intentions differ from yours, and it is difficult for us to say that one is "good" and one is "bad" -- they are different. And all of us believe (smiling) that we are right, do we not? And so, those who oppose us are "obviously" wrong -- since they cannot be right, too, if we are right -- but what it comes down to is that WE ARE NOT RIGHT OR WRONG -- WE ARE DIFFERENT. And we have evolved, as beings, to the point of knowing that we hold. And you may trust the point of knowing that you are currently at, by the way that you feel.

Now, in regards to your specific question about the "channeling of entities, or nonphysical beings."

For the most part, the connection that you make will be a being who is of your "Family of Consciousness." It is very unusual that you would attract one whose intentions were not in harmony with your own.

However, as with all things that we have talked about, here tonight, anything that you give great thought to, you will create. And so, if you have tremendous fear of that, it is possible that you may, very well, attract that which you fear most, for the Creative Process works evenly to all things.

And so, because there have been those who have had such experiences, and as they talk about them to others, they spread the fear. You see? It is an unnatural thing that they have created, but as they stimulate the thoughts in others, which brings forth fear, then the others create it as well.

And so, then, someone has to do something to compensate for that, and so, then, they say, "If you will say these things, and touch your face in these different ways, you will cast away all evil spirits." (Group laughter) You see? And if there is BELIEF that those things work, then the "evil spirits" no longer come to you. You see?

There is never a reason for you to create anything in your experience that you are not wanting.

And here is the most powerful line of the evening.

YOU INVITE ALL THROUGH YOUR THOUGHT.

And so, if you're not "knowing that evil spirits exist," you would never invite them, because you would not think about them. But as they are talked about, you think about them, and you may invite them -- if you are in the process of allowing. Now this is the tricky part, and it is what makes it so unusual for anyone to have that sort of experience. Truthfully, most of those experiences are imagined, or made up. They do not really happen, most of them, for this reason:

Everything that you experience, you must give thought to, or as we say, "IN DELIBERATE CREATING, YOU MUST WANT IT -- AND THEN ALLOW IT TO BE." And so, in this process of "channeling," the "wanting" is set forth by saying, "I would like to have communication with the inner dimension." And as we have talked about, here this evening, be specific:

"I am wanting a joyous communication. I AM WANTING TO SPEAK WITH THOSE BEINGS THAT ARE IN HARMONY WITH WHO I AM, WHO WILL UPLIFT ME. I AM WANTING A HIGH LEVEL OF CONSCIOUSNESS, for I am understanding that there are many frivolous beings, and I am not communicating for fun, so much as I am for knowing."

Make your statement so that you set forth the creation in the way that you are wanting. And then, as you sit to "meditate," you will ALLOW it, for your intention, as you "meditate," is to open the channel of communication. You see?

Most beings who are afraid of "evil spirits" never have the experience, for they will not allow the communication. They will never sit, intending to receive communication, for they are so afraid that they will receive something that is evil, that they do not *allow* it. And that is the reason that we say most of those stories are made up -- it is not in harmony with the Creative Process. You see?

Both the wanting and the allowing must be in place before the experience...You hear so many things.

WE ENCOURAGE YOU TO PAY VERY LITTLE ATTENTION TO ANYONE WHO TELLS YOU ANYTHING

ABOUT ANYTHING, BUT TO *MAKE YOUR DECISIONS BASED UPON YOUR OWN LIFE EXPERIENCE* -- AND WEIGH IT AGAINST THE WAY THAT YOU FEEL AS YOU ARE HAVING THE EXPERIENCE, FOR YOU DO NOT UNDERSTAND THE INTENT OF THE PERSON WHO AT-TRACTED THEIR EXPERIENCE. It may very well be that that being knew, very well, the process of communication, already knew all of the possibilities, and wanted that sort of experience, and deliberately attracted it.

When we tell you that we are not aware of beings who are manifesting into the physical, instantly, we tell you that, because it is not occurring.

There are those who are manifesting, instantly, through their thought, but not that that others can see. And if you are hearing otherwise, it is such a story as we have described. Until you meet one who has seen....

Esther has said, "Abraham, you are wise, and you are powerful, can we not have some magic, just to stimulate the thought of those who do not believe? Could we not create something; perhaps a diamond would be nice?" (Laughter)

And we have said, "What keeps the nonbeliever from saying that you have slipped it out of your sleeve, as all magicians do?"

And she said, "Oh yes, you are right, it must be bigger. Let us have an elephant." (Laughter)

And then we said, "Have you not seen an elephant appear upon a stage?"

JERRY: Siegfried and Roy (an illusion act in Las Vegas, Nevada.)

ABRAHAM: Indeed. There is nothing that a nonbeliever will believe until they are *wanting* to believe.

And so, if we set about, trying to turn nonbelievers into believers, then we defeat our own intent, for our intent is to interact with those who are seeking? You see? Not to attract those who want to be entertained with magic.

QUESTION: How do I keep my vision, or thoughts, under control -- what is the best way...?

ABRAHAM: The best way is to make more decisions, in every day, about what you DO want, and to be sensitive to your warning bells. We have stated that many times.

COMMENT: I know. (Laughs)

ABRAHAM: We are not beating up on you. It is that it is such a simple thing that it is hard to believe.

You are living in a complex society, and you are believing that something, so important, must be much more difficult -- and that something that simple, must have something wrong with it.

COMMENT: Maybe if we'd make all of this more complex, we'd remember.

ABRAHAM: That is precisely why we speak so many hours. (Group laughter) It is the reason that you make more out of *everything* -- in order to substantiate.

You see, you feel you must justify everything because you do not believe that you are worthy. You do not understand who you are, and so you have built a world around yourselves to justify your existence.

And what we are wanting you to understand, is that you don't need to justify your existence, you "are" because you wanted to be.

Love yourselves as you are, and now make up your mind what you want from here, and do it.

Now we will give you something else to chew on: Whenever you are justifying -- you are miscreating. What do you think about that?

COMMENT: I believe you.

ABRAHAM: Now, we will tell you why: When you are in the mode of justification, you are trying to convince yourself that something "should be" that you do not believe is. The emotion that is present when you are justifying is always negative emotion -- and you are trying to convince yourself otherwise.

Don't justify anything. Say you want it because you want it, and that is reason enough. And if someone is putting you in a corner, badgering you, asking for justification -- tell them that you want it because you want it. Give them something to chew on.

QUESTION: When you say, "I want this," and the other person says, "Well, I am just being realistic," what is a good comeback to them?

ABRAHAM: What is your intent in "coming back?" That is what you first must ask yourself. To stimulate them to the knowing that you have come to?

This is what you would say:

"I have come to know that my realism holds me right here, for if I will only allow what is presently real in my experience, then I will never grow beyond it. And so, I have decided to forget about current reality and to think about future reality. And the future holds much more for me than the present, for I am getting better at creating every day."

And the one who is seeking will say, "What?"

And then you will say, "Are you wanting to know what I know about this?"

"Indeed."

"Well, what I have discovered is that my thoughts create, and I know that sounds crazy. The first time I heard it I thought it was crazy, but then I started paying attention to what I was thinking -- and what I was getting. And I was amazed to find that they were the same.

"As I looked at my life, I had to admit that what I thought about was there, everywhere. And as I looked at other people around me, I started noticing a correlation there, too. What they talked about was in their experience.

"My mother speaks of ill health, continually, and has more of it than anyone that I know. And so, I decided that maybe there was something to it, and while I don't understand it, and in the beginning I didn't really believe it, I decided to be open to the possibility. What if it is true and I am missing something?

"And so, I began projecting my thoughts, and I began receiving. I am not saying it was all easy, for in the beginning, the more I thought the more I thought. And I recognized that it was not always a happy finding -- and that I was doing it ALL to myself.

"It was disappointing when I found that I couldn't blame the others, for I was enjoying, very much, blaming it on everyone else, but when I really understood that I was the one, the feeling of blame was replaced with a feeling of ecstasy, for in knowing that I am the creator, I found freedom. Freedom to be who I am, but more importantly, freedom to let them be who they are, for I know that I do not invite them into my experience unless I think about them. And when I recognized that they couldn't get in without my invitation, then I stopped worrying about them. I stopped fearing the robber; I stopped fearing the rapist; I stopped fearing everything that I had feared before, because I realized that it would not come in and get me -- unless I invited it with my thought.

"In the beginning I felt overwhelmed because to think about my thoughts was very cumbersome, there were too many of them. To control my every thought was absolutely impossible, but then I found that there was this wonderful correlation between what I was thinking and how I was feeling. And my feelings were much more easy to discern.

"I discovered that when I am feeling good, I am creating good, and when I am feeling bad, I am creating bad. And so I decided I will feel good. And when I feel bad I will say, 'Why am I feeling bad? What am I thinking?' Identify what it is, release it, and think of what I want instead.

"I have told you the secrets that I have learned, my friend. Go forth, and experience, and see if they don't work for you."

And they will say, "What?" (Group laughter)

The first time that you are hearing this, it is not easy to hear because of the patterns that we have talked about. Because of the lifetime of blaming others. And so, out of habit, your first instinct is to say, "I have not done this. Someone else has."

As long as you are blaming somebody else you will not understand the Creative Process.

February 3, 1988

QUESTION: In this physical experience we have the opportunity to vote for things that we want, like abortion and capital punishment, and things which take another life. How...do we go? By our inner feelings?

ABRAHAM: We would encourage you to let your *inner feelings* guide you. Your inner feelings come forth from a broader perspective. You have intended to be allowers. You see, the only reason that you feel that you need to protect yourself from others is because you don't understand that they can't get into your experience without your invitation, through thought. When you really understand that another -- no matter what their intentions and no matter how close they are -- cannot invade your experience, then you don't feel the need for those things.

It is tricky business, for you have many laws, earthly laws that we call agreements, and we are in favor of agreements. For there are many things -- such as everyone understanding that the red light means stop and the green light means go -- that make your coexistence more comfortable. And there are many agreements that you have entered into so that you may move about more comfortably.

But it is also our knowing that many of your laws have been created out of fear, and when you focus upon anything that has been created out of fear, then you begin to attract that very thing into your life experience -- and so, then you need more laws. And so, then you create more laws, which cause more thought and more focus and more attention to it -- and then you need more laws.

You see, the laws of this country...And many of you were part of those beginning legislations, for many of you were part of the beginning of this country. It was your last physical experience here. Your laws were much more simple than they are now...But as you have initiated laws which attract attention you attract more of that which needs more laws, and that is why your laws have gotten broader and broader and broader and broader. (Pause)

As you are intending that which you want, it makes little difference what laws are passed around you.

QUESTION: Do we ever come into a physical lifetime, and due to circumstances, stagnate? I know that we receive new experience, and from that, we receive growth and perspective which we take with us, but from a point of view, it seems like, for myself, and for many people I've talked to, there has been a very remarkable uplifting during this last few years and in our lifetime, and do we ever experience a lifetime where that does not occur?

ABRAHAM: Most of your lifetime is stagnation. More is than is not. And the reason for it is because of the influence of others.

As you are born into this physical experience, you are much more clearly focused in your inner perspective than you are your conscious physical perspective. As that infant, you are not physically focused at all. You are remembering, very much, why you are here, and you are feeling invincible. There is nothing that you do not believe that you will accomplish, that you have intended. But as you are here longer and longer, you begin to hear the words and see the life experience of those who surround you, and through a process of absorption -- it is not really, for you are receiving and creating within your own life experience, the beliefs -- *but you begin to absorb, literally, the beliefs of those who surround you, and as you absorb their beliefs, you do not create anything that has not already been experienced.* You talk about the same things that have already been talked about. You regurgitate beliefs, over and over again, not reaching for the new. And if you should try to reach for the new, they usually grab you and drag you back, for they are not wanting you to express or experience something that is new, for they are seeking the comfort of sameness, for the most part, because, for the most part, they do not understand the Creative Process, or the intent or even the existence of the broader being.

There was a time when you understood, even more clearly than you do now, the vastness of your being, but over a period of many, many, many, many lifetimes, physical man has begun to suppress his Inner Being.

And now, you are reawakening. It is a glorious time that is before you. For as you find points of harmony with your Inner Being, it is your greatest point of physical pleasure, as well.

The greatest physical pleasure that you experience, is always in perfect harmony with the intentions of your Inner Being -- and there is not an exception to that. And your greatest points of negative emotion are always your greatest points of disharmony with your inner intentions. And you may trust those feelings. There is not another that you may trust as clearly.

February 6, 1988

TALK SHOW HOST: Our guest is Abraham, being channeled through Esther Hicks. This is K..., talk radio, back to the phones in a moment.

(off the air)

(on the air)

HOST: 9 minutes until eleven o'clock. I'm...(host of talk show) Esther Hicks is here, and here comes Abraham. Let's go to the telephones. Thanks for waiting, and you're on K... And I think Abraham is ready to talk again.

CALLER: OK, I just wanted to ask Abraham what I can do to improve my self- esteem? (very flat voice tones)

ABRAHAM: Let us give you some words first, and then we will give you some specific techniques, but hear this:

You are a perfect being, as you are. Not perfect in the sense that you are finished, for there is not an ending to growth, but perfect in the sense that as you are, is good. You see, it is only in this physical life experience where there is continual comparison of one to another...And always the point of comparison is to find something better than the other, and there is no value in this comparison, for there are not two who are the same...You are not the same in your physical sense, but if you could see yourself from your broader sense, from the totality of your being, then you would know how very much different you are from every other thing in the universe. Understand that as you are is a culmination of all that you have experienced in this life experience, and that it is good. It is all right.

Now hear this: You have done the most important part of creating that which you are wanting. You have said, "How can I have this?" which is a strong indication that you are wanting it. And that is the first part, and the most important part, of setting any creation in motion: Want it. "I am wanting to have more self esteem." And now you have only to allow it.

At the beginning of every day, take a paper and pencil and write at the top of it, "I am wanting to be more sure of myself. I am wanting to draw those life experiences that will assist me in that."

Now this is going to sound strange to you, for you may not have heard it before, but trust that the power of the universe will give to you, life experience that will enhance that which you are asking for. Expect it, for we are expecting it for you. There will be much assistance for you. You have set it into motion with your words and with your thought, and it will be.

CALLER: Thank you very much.

HOST: Thanks for calling. Abraham, it sounds like you and Dr. Norman Vincent Peale used to work together. Do you pay attention to other people here on the old planet?

ABRAHAM: We are aware of some. Not of all. We are aware of this one that you speak of.

You see, as we are gathered together here, we are drawn by intent, and the being of whom you speak, his Inner Being dwells *here* with Abraham, and so, the physical being that he has evolved to has evolved to that point because he has responded to the urging that has come forth from his Inner Being. We are of the same "Family," you might say.

HOST: You all went to different schools together?

ABRAHAM: MMMMmmmmmm, more or less.

HOST: From North Dallas, you're on K...

CALLER: I have a couple of things to say and a question to ask. (Pained voice)

HOST: Well give us one thing to say and one question, because we are running close to the hour.

CALLER: OK. Well, I'm only 35 years old but I've had neck surgery and discs out, and....and I realized that I had done something wrong...past life in Korea, and I developed problems and stuff in my lower back, and so I'm wondering if it's "Karma" connected. And if it's "Karma" connected, do I have to work it out and live with chronic pain, or can I set it straight?

ABRAHAM: It is a wonderful question. Know that it is not connected to anything in a past life. There is not any of that. *You are experiencing, in this life experience, only that which you have created through the thoughts that you have set forth within this life experience.*

And now, let us talk about you now, for you are in great pain, are you not?

CALLER: I am, really. I have also had a lifetime in martial arts. I'm still trying...

ABRAHAM: Let us give you something that will assist you a great deal. For as you have been listening here -- have you been hearing the words that we've offered so far?

CALLER: Yes, I've listened carefully.

ABRAHAM: As you are setting thoughts into motion, you will receive that which you are wanting, but there has already been some damage done to your physical apparatus, and so, it is...

When your toe is throbbing it is very difficult to think about a healthy foot.

And so, what we are encouraging you to do, is, before you go to sleep at night, right before you go to sleep, to set a very strong statement of intent, in this way: "I am intending perfect health." Do not say,"I am wanting to be free of pain," that will draw your attention to it, but see yourself free of the pain, absent of the pain. See yourself in perfect health, and if you will do it right before you sleep, then there will be many hours where you will be unconscious, where you will not be doing any miscreating to counteract that. And if you will do it in every night for the next 30 or 40 or maybe even 60 days, you will find a great improvement in what you are currently experiencing.

CALLER: Can I reverse the damage done to the apparatus?

ABRAHAM: You can.

CALLER: I certainly appreciate it.

ABRAHAM: Indeed.

March 1, 1988

COMMENT: Since you recommended earlier that we have the shift questions first, I'll ask one.

ABRAHAM: That was Esther's recommendation..

142

(Group laughs)

COMMENT: Thank you Abraham, I apologize. To keep Esther happy, I shall ask this question.

ABRAHAM: It is good to keep her happy. She threatens at times to hold her mouth shut, and it is very difficult to speak under those conditions.

QUESTION: Should we be so concerned about being in a safe place -- or should we just be more concerned about going on about our lives doing what we feel like we're supposed to be doing?

ABRAHAM: That is the best thing to do, for as you focus upon that which troubles you, you attract the trouble itself, you see. Truly it is enough if you say, "I intend joyous survival." You see, it is the reason that we are wanting to stimulate the thoughts of those who are in areas...whether they are areas of safety or whether they are not areas of safety. For it is of value to bring to the conscious knowing that there is something that may happen. It is only a probability in the minds of most, and not a very great probability in the minds of most, for it is outside of your conscious experience, you see.

And so, as you are stimulated to the probability, if all it does for you is bring you to the conscious decision, "I intend to survive this," then that is enough. For you will be at the right place at the right time -- if you are wanting to continue physical experience.

What we are not wanting to occur, is that, for some reason, a being be caught totally unaware so that they have not had an opportunity to make a conscious decision about what it is that they choose, you see.

And whenever you are surprised by something, you respond to it, (but) usually not in the direction of your dominant intention.

You see, your action always follows the course of your

dominant intention, and the reason that we encourage you to intend, segment by segment, what you are wanting, is so that your dominant intention will be uppermost on your mind, so that when something occurs, no matter what it is, that you will not be caught off guard.

Your dominant intention has already been decided. But if you have not intended anything about this segment and something occurs that catches you off guard, then you are swept up by the influence of others, you see -- and you may create in a direction that is not really to your wanting.

In this time there will be much panic. There will be many who are caught off guard, and they will stimulate one another negatively. And they will create negatively, simply because there will be wide-spread panic, you see? But for those who have decided ahead of time what they intend for this segment, when it occurs, their intentions will be clear and strong, and they will immediately be creating that, you see.

And so, you are correct. *To tend with the details of anything that you are setting into motion, is usually where your greatest miscreating occurs,* and so, we encourage all of you to step back, in the beginning, and say, "I intend joyous creation. I intend joyous creative survival. I intend harmony. I intend to eat well and be warm and be surrounded by those that I am harmonious with." And as you set those intentions in motion, then you will begin attracting the circumstances and other thoughts which will bring it about and bring the detail of it into clearer focus for you, you see.

As you try to deal with the details of that which is so vague and so far away, like, "What will I do for work, or what will I do for money," those sorts of things, it is too far away for you to think about that, you see. But as you try, (To deal with the unknown details) because you don't have enough information, currently, that is where your miscreating begins to occur. That is where fear comes in. That is when you start worrying. And fear or worry is a signal that you are miscreating, you see.

And so, your advice to all is very good. Go about your joyous experience, intending some more of it, you see. That is what we recommend, indeed.

What more?

QUESTION: Abraham, is this my imagination, or...I'm sensing changing in our weather, right now?

ABRAHAM: What you are sensing is the event drawing nearer. All of you are sensing it.

As we are together tonight, let us talk about a specific method for you to be clearer about knowing the timing of this event, for it is what we are hearing from all of you. "We are wanting to know when it is, Abraham? Could you give us a date?"

We are wanting to know specifically when it is, as well, and we are anticipating that it is not far, but it is not an easy thing to know. But there is not a great deal of value about preparing for it, after it is too late. And so, we are encouraging immediate preparation, so that you will be ready for it beforehand, for it is certainly an immediate possibility, from what we are sensing.

Now, there are a number of things: Your animals are very sensitive to it, and if you have an animal, or have access to being near one, pay attention to their habits. And you will notice a nervousness abut them increasing as it is getting nearer. The reasons that the animals are apparent in their warning is because they are operating from a purer Inner Being than you are. You consciously resist.

You may be having much unconscious warning coming forth from the Inner Being, but there is conscious resistance, you see. And your consciousness is more powerful than that which comes forth from within. That is why you don't trust yourself as you are receiving information that comes forth from within, because, consciously, you cannot prove it, you see.

And so, your animals, because they do not have this conscious overriding, are responding continually to what they are feeling, and so, if you don't trust yourself, watch them. But what we are encouraging each of you to do, is to recognize and accept the fact that you are receiving clear communication from your Inner Being in the form of emotion.

Now, whether you ever believe a word that comes through your thinking mechanism, or not, you cannot deny the validity of the emotion that comes through. And so, if you are wanting to strengthen your belief in your ability to communicate with your Inner Being, then ask questions that can be answered in a "yes" or "no" fashion, with negative emotion meaning, "no," and positive emotion meaning "yes," and put yourself in a position where you are saying, "I am wanting to know, at this time, the safety of the area in which I stand. Specifically, I am not wanting to know if this building will fall down, I will ask that later. I am wanting to know if generally, if comparatively, in comparison with that which is upon the earth, is this place where I now sit, a place of safety, or a place of danger -- with safety being indicated by positive emotion and danger being indicated by negative emotion."

And if you are wanting, now, we will help you to receive that. Put your feet on the floor, your hands in your lap, and as you are an open being, having already opened the passageway, you will receive this emotion very keenly. If you receive nothing, don't worry about it, we will tell you what to do about that later. And so, here it is. We are asking that the Inner Being that is within each of us will come forth in the form of emotion and let us know the comparative safety of this area in which we are now all currently sitting. (pause)

It is all right is it not? Even some goose bumps here or there, you see.

(Group smiling. Almost all had positive response..)

As you are open, you may ask for nodding if you are wanting, but you don't always trust the nodding. The emotion is harder to deny.

Now project yourself...let us go to San Diego. And we are setting forth the same question. We are asking, from our Inner Being, specific guidance about the safety of the area of San Diego. (12 second pause)

That is enough. Esther is about to vomit. (to those nearest) Don't worry, she really won't. (group laughter) But it is the way that she is feeling, for the emotion is very powerful. And what did you receive? (to group)

Now, any place that you are wondering about, as you project yourself there, you will know, a very clear indication.

QUESTION: I'd like to talk about prayer, if we could, a little bit. Jesus, I understand, healed people by seeing them, when they were supposedly ill, as whole and perfect. And their faith made them well?

ABRAHAM: Absolutely.

QUESTION: Now, can we do that same thing for other people?

ABRAHAM: Indeed. When your belief is powerful enough, and you are able to transmit -- through your power of influence -- your belief within another.
All healing is done by the individual. I cannot heal you, but I can convince you that there is healing for you, and if you will accept that it can be, then it can be, you see. And so, the more certain I am about the ability to heal, then the more influential I may be to you.

JERRY: And so, what's the best way to never have to be healed?

ABRAHAM: The best situation regarding all things, not only health, but all creation, is to create that which you are wanting, so that you don't have to go back and uncreate it, or create something that you prefer. But that is really not a very possible thing, for you are a changing being. In other words, it would be very easy for us to say, "It is better never to get sick in the first place than to have to deal with illness after you've got it," but then that would apply to everything in the universe, would it not? It would be better never to make a mistake, then you would never have to correct it. But knowing comes forth from that, and so there is no value in regret or no value in beating up on yourself. No value in saying, "Oh, look at this thing that I have done to myself in my miscreating, I have created illness." You see? It is much better to say, "I know now how it is that I have created it, and now what I choose, instead, is perfect health."

You can use your miscreating to your great advantage if you will allow it to be proof to you of your ability to create. The sickest of beings is the most magnificent of creators, for they have used the power of thought, more specifically than most other beings that you know, to create. And just because it is something that they do not want is not reason to not like oneself or not trust oneself. It is reason to say, "Look what powerful creator I am."

JERRY: So health is natural, and anything beyond that is something we have created, beyond what we already have?

ABRAHAM: Your natural state of being is a state of joy, and a state of health, and a state of growth. Now, that does not mean that every being coming into this physical expression is looking at it from that point of view, for as they have been evolving through lifetimes, physical and nonphysical, they have some new intentions, but the natural state of being is that.

COMMENT: Abraham, in one of your classes that I attended, you really helped me a lot. Well, you've helped me an awful lot in a lot of ways, but this one way, I think about all the time: When you said..."Whatever you focus on the most is what you draw into your creation."

I had a friend walk up to me the other day...all crippled with arthritis, working in a nursing home for about 15 years. That's all she thinks about is the old people with arthritis. She even has her husband building a new home...making sure the doors on her bathroom will accommodate a wheelchair, in case she might need it some day.

ABRAHAM: She will.

QUESTION: Yes, and so, being an old X-ray technician, I'm so glad that I'm not working any more in that career because I'd be creating all of that.

So, I was listening to one of your tapes the other day...when you said that...Esther and Jerry were creating a first aid box..and then all of a sudden...they began hurting themselves...Did they draw that into their existence because they were focusing on the first aid box?

ABRAHAM: Absolutely. The thought of a need, drew.

COMMENT: This, I want you to know, has really helped me a lot in my life, in knowing what I don't want to focus on, career wise, for my husband, my family, for what I'm doing. It's a wonderful thing to be able to see. Someone that has worked in a nursing home, and focused on that, is going to draw the death that much faster to them?

ABRAHAM: It does not need to be that way. It is possible to work in a nursing home, dealing with beings who are sick and crippled, and saying to yourself in every day, "I am assisting these in the relief of suffering of that which they have created. And I have no intention of creating anything within my being other than health."

COMMENT: But your average, everyday person doesn't know this.

ABRAHAM: That is correct.

QUESTION: And so, what they do, is they create it by default?

ABRAHAM: You are right.

QUESTION: Can you intend something for someone else?

ABRAHAM: You cannot. *If you are wanting another to understand what you understand, (then) through your strong intent, and your power of influence, you may stimulate their thought, and as you stimulate the thought within them, then they* *may begin to attract it in their experience. That is what we call good influence or bad influence.*

If there is a friend who continually talks of sickness, and you willingly listen, acting as a sounding board, then you are a negative influence, for you encourage negative creating, but if, instead, you only speak of health, you only speak of prosperity, you only speak of those things that you are wanting in your experience, then you are an influence for that which you consider good, you see.

You are correct. Most beings do not understand that, and so, out of habit, and out of widespread influence, they stimulate one another to negative creating, and then they think that it is outside of self, you see, for they wouldn't have done it on purpose, and so someone else must have done it.

COMMENT: I wanted to tell this lady, "Get out of that nursing home. Look at your fingers already. You're already creating this, ten years down the line..."

ABRAHAM: There is something in what you have said that can be of value in another area that touches you in every day. And that is the area of relationships with other people.

As you recognize that you literally attract from life with your thought...you attract sickness, you attract health, you attract prosperity, you attract poverty, you attract good relationships, you attract bad relationships -- all through your thought. Now, if you can break it down a little bit finer and recognize, that in every being that you interact with, there is some of all of that. There is some of that which you want, and some of that which you do not want.

Even your greatest enemy has more points of harmony than of disharmony, and so, as you are wanting to interact with a being that you are not getting along with, with a being that rings your warning bells continually, if you will intend to see that which you approve of, if you intend to see that which you like, then you will literally begin to solicit from that being, those things.

Jokes
neighbors

COMMENT: Because you are attracting only what you see, right?

ABRAHAM: Esther was watching the television before you came. The subject was racial discrimination. And new understanding came to Esther.

Racial discrimination is created by the being who feels abused. By the being who believes that he is being treated unfairly. And that belief, that expectation, attracts it out of beings who otherwise would never be racialists. Most beings have never given it a thought, for it is not something that they have interacted with at all.

But because there is this belief that "Because I am a certain color I am mistreated," then as I walk the streets, I solicit that from every being with whom I interact. But I do not know that I am doing it through my thought, you see, and so I blame you. I blame you because you look at me strangely, and I think you don't like me because I am not the color that you are, you see. And it has nothing to do with you. I have solicited it from you, through my thought. Do you see? Are you understanding this? Are you understanding that every relationship you have -- whenever you are having unpleasant experiences, you are attracting the unpleasant experience because that is where you are giving your attention.

We will give you an example, and then we will hear from you. Have you ever known someone, you meet them, they are outside of the environment in which they have grown up, they are away at school, not in the town where they were raised, not near their mother, or their father, or anyone that has known them, and as you meet this being, it is a perfect specimen of humanity. As far as you are concerned, it is a wondrous being. And as you look at this wondrous being with that attitude, the being becomes more wondrous every day. You just can't believe that you have met such a marvelous person. And then that person takes you home, and the mother of that person begins to tell you of all of the things that person did while they were growing up, pointing out all of the weaknesses, all of the things that have been overcome, or need to be overcome, and suddenly you are looking at that person in a new light. And suddenly you say, "Yes, I see that, I can see how you aren't as strong as I thought you were, and not as smart as I thought you were." And as you look at that being with that new set of intentions, you begin to solicit from them that which you do not like, and then you say, "I don't really want to be with you. I am looking for a perfect one." *It is the reason that most relationships deteriorate:*

When you are drawn together, you are drawn together by that which you are wanting, you see, but then as you are together, your focus is no longer on what is wanted...but upon what is not wanted.

Here is the principle, for it will apply regarding all things. You see in this being all the things that you are wanting until you are influenced by another to see the flaws. As you are influenced by another, or even by your own habit -- you may always look for flaws -- as you are influenced by, whatever, others or your own habits, to look for the flaws, then you begin to solicit, to summon, to literally draw from that being, the things that you don't like. Where before, before the influence, you were drawing the things that you did like. Do you understand what we are saying?

The "imperfect" or the "perfect" person has nothing to do with it. Just as all of the beings in the nation who are being accused of racialism or of racial discrimination are not the ones that are creating it. It is being created by the one who feels that he is prejudiced against.

QUESTION: OK. Now this person here, you're seeing all of these imperfections, and you are literally drawing them out of him?

ABRAHAM: Indeed. He is becoming your creation.

QUESTION: OK. The more you draw, the more you dislike. Now you are going to treat him this way. Now, is it his fault you're treating him that way?

ABRAHAM; You are seeing that which you are intending. He is as he always has been. He is as everything and everyone is, a combination of all of these things, you see. But you are drawing from him -- just as you draw from life -- that which you focus upon.

And if you focus upon that which you are wanting to see, that is what you will draw into your experience -- whether you are talking about the entire universe, or one single soul.

COMMENT: All right. I understand that part. But I don't understand...

COMMENT: May I offer an analogy. Something that happened to me not very long ago. I was at a friend's house, in the front yard, and this rather aggressive dog comes trotting up, you know. I happen to like animals very much, and I said a few words to the dog, and it wagged it's tail and went on. Two seconds later a lady appears across the street to go get her garbage cans, and she sees the dog and immediately reacts negatively, and the dog goes after her. Same dog.

ABRAHAM: Indeed. It is a perfect analogy.

QUESTION; These people can have these imperfections in them?

ABRAHAM: Indeed. There is not one who does not.

QUESTION: But we can either allow it or not?

ABRAHAM: Your relationship with them depends upon your ability to focus upon what you want.
(Dog barks from outside, very loud. Group laughs)

COMMENT: That's what you call having the last say.

ABRAHAM: It is indeed. (Group laughs)

QUESTION: What I was asking is, what you draw from that person, I understand that part, now...

ABRAHAM: Let us interrupt before you go any further. *The tendency is to blame the other for his imperfection.*

We are wanting you to assume the responsibility for his imperfection as he interacts with you, for you are soliciting it from him. The tendency is to see a flaw in another and judge and blame the other, and what we are saying to you is -- only what you see is there.

And so, now where are you? Now you are in a position where you may have perfect relationships with everyone as you are clear about what you are wanting and as you are only seeing what you are wanting. And when you see that which is not in harmony with who you are, look away. When your warning bell rings because that which you are seeing is not in harmony with what you are wanting, turn your attention to something else, you see.

What you are most wanting to understand in this life experience is this: It is the greatest intention that you have, and we speak it forcefully: *You are wanting to be ALLOWERS. And you will know when you have achieved that when you are willing to allow another, even when the other does not allow you. When you are able to allow, even when the other is not allowing you -- you will have absolute freedom.*

You see, the only thing that binds you is negativity. Without it you are free, joyously. And so, as you look at another and see only that which brings forth joy -- you are free. As you look at another and see that which brings forth negativity -- you are bound by your own decision of what you are soliciting.

We are wanting you to release the responsibility from all those you are blaming for all of the things they are doing wrong and for all of the ways they are messing up your life. They are not doing it! You are doing it!

COMMENT: That is deep stuff. (Group laughter)

ABRAHAM: It is the deepest of the stuff. (Group laughter) And it is the most meaningful words that you will hear as you are moving forward, for you are interacting with others, and it applies not only to the others, my friends -- it applies to your own being.

You solicit from your very own being that which you do not want to be. You look at yourself, and you see that which is wrong. You see that which is not in harmony with your greater wanting, and as you do it -- you create more.

See in yourselves that which you are wanting, and that is what you will draw forth. Do you see? Indeed you do. That is very good. Did you write it down? (To Jerry)

JERRY: I put, "Transcribe this. This is deep stuff." (Group laughter)

ABRAHAM: What more?

QUESTION: How do you learn to separate, in your own mind, actual truth and knowledge from sheer perception.

ABRAHAM: There is a difference? You see, we are looking for the beginning point of this, for it is another very good question, and very broad subject. It is, perhaps, what we hear the most concern about. For you are wanting to do that which is truth. You are wanting to find that which is good. But you are not knowing where to look for it. Who to trust? Who has the truth? There is so much diversity in what is believed to be truth, that it is usually a lifelong search, and it is never certain that it has been found, you see.

Your question was very well worded, and our answer to you is that *"truth" can only be that which is perceived to be true in any point in time.*

If this house were on fire and the men with the fire truck and the water were to come and open the door and put the water in the house and extinguish the fire, everyone would say that is a most wondrous thing. The "truth" is, that is good. But if, in the same way, the men were to come and open the door and put their hoses in and put the water in, but there was no fire, then everyone would say, the "truth" of this is, that was not so good, you see? When it was the same thing. It was just a different time, different intentions, different reasons, different knowing, different understanding, different circumstances.

And so, if you will accept that all life experience is good. All! All! We are not wanting to shout, but ALL LIFE EXPERIENCE IS GOOD! Then you will understand that there is truth in every experience, and it is a changing thing as experiences and wanting and understanding change. Do you see?

You come from a culture that has been born into a set of beliefs that...say, "There are a set of rules, and these things are good and these things are bad." And it is not that way.

You see, as you are looking for your truth outside of yourself, hearing it through the words of others, you will always have that question, for you will hear many different answers, *but as you are looking for that truth from that which comes from within you, then you will never question it, for your Inner Being knows the truth that is appropriate for you -- and you may trust it.*

And so, when you are feeling positive emotion, you are moving toward that which is perfect for you, in this time. When you are feeling negative emotion, you are moving away from that which is good for you, you see?

QUESTION: Say something about "guilt"?

ABRAHAM: *Guilt is negative emotion, and it comes forth, usually, when you are not doing what someone else has told you that you should do.*

The rule says: "This is good, and this is bad," and so, when you do that, you get guilt. Not because it is bad, but because you think that you are doing that which is not good, and your Inner Being is saying, "Not so." You are not in harmony with your greater intent -- which is to have experience, you see?

That is "deep stuff" too. (Group laughter) There are many that would run kicking and screaming from the room at the hearing of those words, for they are so convinced that there are sets of rules that must be followed, but if they will say, and know the meaning of it, "I am a joy seeking being," and then they will recognize the way they feel about that -- perhaps they will come to understand.

Guilt

QUESTION: If I'm having growth through negative experience, since I intended the joyful experience and I'm getting negativity, then I'm going against harmony?

ABRAHAM: You are. Pay attention to the way that you feel,
and when you feel good, know that you are in harmony and
moving toward that which you are intending. Negative emotion
means you are miscreating.
    Simple, is it not? *Any time you don't feel good, stop
doing whatever you are doing.* Now, hear this: We are wanting
to clarify this. We will state it again. ANY TIME YOU ARE
NOT FEELING GOOD, STOP DOING WHATEVER IT IS
YOU ARE DOING. Now, you must understand, it is the
thought -- in the moment -- that brings forth the negative emotion.
    Now this is very important, we must take a moment
here. We've been upon the topic of guilt. "My mother has told
me that if I do not go to church, I will burn in hell. She believes
it. I want to please her. She thinks I have gone to church, but I
have not. I have gone to play. I am filled with guilt."
    The guilt is coming forth, not because I am at play and
not at church. The guilt is coming forth because I am thinking
that I am doing that which is wrong, and the Inner Being is
saying, "That is not in harmony."
    The reason we have clarified this is because we say to
you, "When you feel negative emotion, stop what you are doing," and so, you jump to the conclusion that you must stop not
going to church, for that is what has brought forth this feeling.
That is not what has brought forth the feeling. When you didn't
go to church you were excited about it. You were happy about
what you were going to do. Until you thought of your mother,
and her wanting you to be at church, the guilt did not come
forth. Do you see what we are saying? It is your thought that
you are sinning that brings forth the negative emotion, so stop
that thought.
    Do you understand what we are saying? That is where
the confusion about guilt has come forth. Before you can fully
understand this topic, you must first understand that all negative

emotion is communication from your Inner Being, telling you that the THOUGHT that you are thinking is not in harmony with what you are wanting. If you will accept the feeling of "guilt" as a negative emotion telling you that your PRESENT thought is not in harmony with who you are, then you will be closer to understanding why the guilt is coming forth.

If you can release the titles you have given to these negative emotions, such as guilt, jealousy, anger, hate, frustration, anxiety, stress, fear, and recognize that they are all negative warning bells, then it will be easier for you to understand what the warning bell is trying to tell you. In most cases, the feeling of guilt comes forward not because you are doing something "wrong," -- but because your freedom is being suppressed. The warning bell is ringing, not to get you to stop the action you are involved in, not to get you to stop not going to church -- but to let you know that the THOUGHT you are involved in is not in harmony with who you are.

You feel guilty, and they tell you you are guilty because you are sinning. You are not feeling guilty because you are sinning. You are feeling this negative warning bell because they are trying to control you -- and you seek freedom. *You are a being who is here to live and have life experience -- that you may have joyful experiences.*

Guilt does not come forth because you are sinning. Guilt comes forth because of the thought that you are setting forth about that.

Guilt abounds in your culture. It keeps you from liking yourself. And as you feel guilty, you look for more sinful things in yourself. You look for more reasons to feel guilty, you see?

JERRY: As a kid I went to a lot of different churches, and in each church, there were different things I felt guilty about. For instance, in one church, dancing was a sin, but when I went to another church that had different rules (where dancing wasn't sinful) then I didn't feel guilty about dancing in that church where dancing was allowed, and so on. The girls with makeup didn't feel guilty wearing makeup, in the churches where that wasn't considered a sin...

158

ABRAHAM: Perfect, that is what we were reaching for. That is perfect. So the point is, the guilt did not come forth from dancing. The guilt came forth because of the thought of all the different beings in relationship to the dancing. Good. Now that should come back to your question. (To earlier question) "Is the truth something outside of perception?" You see. It is not. Good.
What more?

QUESTION: I've been doing a lot of metaphysical reading lately, and talking to different people, and I keep coming up with this quandary about how to deal with living in this plane while trying to prepare for the next, because it seems like such a conflict. I feel a big need to spend all of my time working towards the next plane and not worrying about this one, but I can't see how that's ever going to work.

ABRAHAM: We are extremely pleased that you have brought this forth, for there is some confusion, and we are wanting to put it to rest, here and now.
You are a physical being in a physical dimension, intending to live on this plane. It is dominant. That which you are thinking and doing here in this focused dimension is that which you are intending to do.
Now, we are encouraging a blending of this conscious physical being with your Inner Being, yes, but not a focus that is taken from here and put somewhere else.
It is most important that you understand that you are in the physical because you have intended to be. Your flesh and bone are proof of that, you see? And so, do not feel that you are focused where it is not meant to be, for you have intended to be focused here, you see.
We encourage, as you are wanting to accomplish the blending -- indeed the awakening that you have so long been hearing about -- we encourage a setting a time aside of 15 or 20 minutes in every day for the allowing of that, but not more, and the rest of your focus, indeed, keep it here, in the here and now, for this is where you are creating, you see. There are many who

do not understand that, and in part it is because they are wanting to escape. They have created that which they do not like, so now they are wanting to get on to something else, and so they are literally focusing outside of their reason for being here, you see. And it does not feel right. Your emotion guides you, you see. Are you clear?

QUESTION: Yes, Would you recommend any specific reading or assignment of any sort?

ABRAHAM: Indeed. We assign you to life! Life experience is that which brings you your knowing. Words, and books, are of great value for they are stimulators of thought, but all that is written is stimulator of thought. One is really not so much better than the other. *Whatever makes you think, so that you will attract life experience, is of value.* We encourage you to set forth your wanting in conscious statement, and that which is appropriate will be attracted.

We will give you some specific information, for it is wanted, and it is of great value. As you are wanting to become this blended being, and indeed you are wanting it, all that is required is that you want it and allow it. *The wanting is easy, it is already done. The allowing is done by setting time aside in every day, 15 or 20 minutes, where you will allow yourself to receive a state of numbness.* Are you knowing what we are meaning by that?

QUESTION: No. Meditation? I've never accomplished it, or really tried.

ABRAHAM: Oh, it is very simple. Let us give you the simple words that will bring it about for you. As you are intending, wanting to accomplish this blending, you have done half of the equation for creation. Want and allow and it is.

The allowing part is accomplished in this way: In every day, set a time aside of 15 or 20 minutes, not more, for the intent is to quiet the physical thinking mind, and if you ask it to be quiet for more than that, it will resist it. 15 or 20 minutes is quite enough. Not one, and then not the next, and then one day, and then not the next. Consistency of a number of days. 20 days will be enough. 20 days, of every day, of sitting for 15 or 20 minutes, will allow the opening of your passageway.

Now, as you are sitting, put your feet on the floor and your hands in your lap, or wherever it is comfortable. Do not lay down, you will go to sleep. Do not sit in too comfortable of a chair, you may go to sleep. And if you go to sleep, you are not doing your work, you see, and so, as you are sitting with the intent of "meditation" -- that is a label we are not liking very much, and so we will tell you what we mean. The intent of this process is to quiet the physical, that you may sense the inner. Which means you must not consciously think. Now, if we say, "Do not think," the first thing you do is think, for you are wanting to think. Your mechanism is trained to think.

And so, as you are sitting quietly in a quiet room with no light or distraction of sound, with your eyes closed, focus upon your breathing, for as you focus upon that which does require thought, but not very much thought, you will quiet your mind. And so, as you breathe out and breathe in and breathe out and breathe in....Have you ever hyperventilated? Taking much oxygen in, leaves you feeling tingly, and it is not so different from that.

If you will allow yourself to breathe very deeply, you will find yourself feeling a little bit tingly, and as you are doing it -- it may be in the first sitting -- you will find yourself feeling a little bit disassociated with what is physical. As you are feeling a little bit numb -- you may not even feel the chair beneath you -- you have done your work.

Now, if it does not occur in the first or second or even the 10th sitting, do not worry about it. Let that be your objective thought. "I am wanting to quiet my mind and I will know my mind is quiet when I have achieved numbness," you see? And as you are feeling this numbness, a sort of tingling, it is different from anything you have known, you will recognize that it is new. Know that you have done your part, and now, your Inner Being will do its part. Your Inner Being, once you have achieved this quieting, will begin the opening of your passage-way. Now it is not really hacking a physical passageway through your being. It is not any physical distress or discomfort. It is an alignment of energy.

You see, every being who is in physical form has the physical body that has been created, that is part of you, but there is an energy that surges through you. That is the difference between the live ones and the dead ones, you see, (Group laughter) and you are accustomed to this energy that surges through you. You have known it since the day you were born, and you say, "This is what it feels like to be alive," you see. But now there is a new energy that will begin to blend with that energy, and that is what this opening of the passageway that we are speaking of is about. And it is not your work. You do not need to consciously know how to do it. You do not need to know what colors the chakras are, and where they are, and what they mean. You have many points of alignment within your being. Do not get involved with it consciously. Let your Inner Being, that knows far more than your conscious mind will ever know about this subject...Let your Inner Being do it. All you must do is quiet your physical. Your Inner Being will do the rest. And as your Inner Being is doing its work, you will be...

Let us begin again. We are putting this in order for you, upon this recording, so that you may listen to it as you are achieving each step. You are understanding what we are saying, and so, your first objective is to sit quietly and achieve the numbness. Once the numbness has been achieved, in however many days it takes to accomplish that, then know that your passageway is being opened, and you will know that it is being opened, you will feel it being opened because you will feel sensations. You will feel a twitch here and a twinge there. Nothing that is painful, but you will say, "Oh, they are working on my nose, I can feel them in my toes." Just a little sensation, and all it is is the new energy that is flowing through you, and you will notice the difference here and there. Once you are receiving movement (head rolling around on neck) your passageway is open. *And once your passageway is open, then there is not a need for this meditation process any more.* Many continue it because they like it.

There are many purposes for meditation. Our purpose,

as it has been expressed here, is for the purpose of opening the passageway. Now what does that mean? When the passageway is open, what does that mean? Does that mean that anything that is out there may pass through it? Indeed it does not. It means that you are opening the passageway between you and you. Your Inner Being, the being that sends forth emotion to you already, will now be able to send, not only clearer emotion, but thought. And it also means -- you will like this very much, (To Questioner: For you are very much not wanting to be a selfish being, it is very important to you that you do your part in all things) -- *you will be benefiting ALL-THAT-IS because once the passageway is open, not only do you benefit by the knowing that comes forth from the inner dimension, but all that is within the inner dimension benefits more clearly by the experience that you are participating within, for the passageway allows information and experience to pass both ways, you see?*

THIS IS LITERALLY THE AWAKENING THAT HAS BEEN TALKED ABOUT. Most beings do not know that it is something for everyone to experience. They think there will be one who will be king, who will have all of the great experience, and the rest will worship, and it is not that way. It is that every being will receive this awakening, this blending of Inner Being and conscious physical being, and as you accomplish this, this physical experience -- in which you are focused, in which you have great intent to be focused, in which you are wanting to be focused -- will be enhanced beyond your conscious understanding in this time. Your physical experience will be more delicious than it has ever been before. Your joy will be ecstasy. Your love will be intense. Your feeling of peace will be beyond anything you have sensed or felt before, you see? All that you experience will be more. Do you see? Your guidance will be keener.

And if you allow it, you will be manifester in a much more dramatic and faster way than ever before.

As you envision that which you want, it will be, more quickly, you see. In your physical life experience there is wondrousness to behold, and it begins with the conscious allowing of the opening of the passageway, you see?

We are appreciative of your question, for it has brought forth, in this discussion, that which is our dominant reason for interacting with those who are physical, you see. To lead you, if it is your wanting, to that.

QUESTION: You said that there are many different reasons for meditation. Once you open the passageway though..I meditate every day because I feel like I need to keep the passageway open.

ABRAHAM: Wanting is enough.

QUESTION: Wanting it is enough, after it's been opened?

ABRAHAM: Anything that has been created, all that is required is that you continue to want it, and it will be.

QUESTION: What would cause it to shut down? Various things?

ABRAHAM: Not wanting it. You see, there is not an ending to any creation. Most of you do not understand that. You create something within your life experience, and once you have got it, then you feel that you no longer need to want it, because now you have it, you see. And so, then you begin wanting other things. *But you must continue to want that which you have created, otherwise it will go away.* Many of you experience that in relationships. You want the relationship. You attract it, and then because you have it, you don't *want* it any more, you see. And then you wonder where it went.

It is true of all things. Start not wanting your automobile, and watch it fall apart. Put your eye upon one you want more, and remove your wanting from the one that you have, and it will disintegrate before your very eyes. As you are looking around at those things that you want, feel your appreciation for them.

Continue to attract that which you want, into your experience. ANYTHING THAT YOU WANT, ATTRACT IT

WITH YOUR THOUGHT, AND AS YOU GIVE THOUGHT TO THAT WHICH YOU DO NOT WANT, YOU WILL AT-TRACT THAT. IT IS LAW.

COMMENT: You know, that is a good law, because you always know where you stand.

ABRAHAM: Indeed, we will keep it then.

QUESTION: I had questions about some of the things I have been reading, and I was hoping to get an opinion from you concerning...

ABRAHAM: Indeed, we are full of opinions. (Group laughter)

QUESTION: I started reading a (metaphysical) book and I have just read the preface of, and I have not gotten into, another (metaphysical) book, and I was just wondering if you had anything to offer regarding those two books?

ABRAHAM: In each of those works that you have spoken of, there is that that we are absolutely in harmony with, and that which we are not in harmony with.

QUESTION: So will I know what I...

ABRAHAM: Indeed you will. That which you feel as you are reading will be your signal to let you know whether it is appropriate to who you are.
   Again we must talk about that which reaches us at any point in time. Your...understanding of the nonphysical dimension, as a people upon the earth, is an evolving thing. The book that you speak of, in fact both books that you speak of, are not currently in absolute harmony with where we are wanting to lead those of you who are in physical form, *but at the time that they were written, they were most appropriate, because of where you were at the time that they were written. Do you see?*

There was a time when you did not...Now, when we say "you," we are speaking of mankind, in physical form, upon planet earth, in general, and that is always tricky business, for you are not the same, but in general -- there was a time when you did not accept the existence of anything that you could not see or smell or touch or taste. If you could not prove it through your physical senses, it did not exist as far as you were concerned. But then enough of you began having experiences, that it...was believed that there was something.

You began to call that something GOD, witches, angels. Then you began to say, "Dead ones can communicate with us," not understanding it, but knowing that there was something that was coming forth from the nonphysical dimension. It was dead Aunt Mary or dead Uncle Bill, willing to participate. No smarter than they ever were, but willing to participate. And then you began to understand that there was guidance coming forth, specific guidance, and so, you began to call them guides.

And now, what we are wanting you to understand is that the guides are not just for one or two selected; the guidance is available to all who are wanting it, and you are not needing to come here for the guidance, it is with you if you will but trust it.

And so, there will be a time when this process, with beings coming here to this woman (Esther) will be something that we will no longer agree with. We will say, "It is not our truth in this time," because what we would rather, is that each of you, individually, bring forth from your own being that which is appropriate. But in this time, most beings do not trust themselves, and so, it is good that you come here for this stimulation for this which you do trust. Do you see what we are saying?

And so, it is a process that is moving forward continually. And it will come to the point where it will not be that you say, "Here I am physical, and (over) here I am from my inner perspective; we are separate." There will come a time when you will say, "I am God. I am Creator." You see? But you are not ready for that yet. Many would cut out the tongue when they hear such a thing, and so, we don't say it very often, (whispering) for most are not ready to hear it, but there will come a time when they will be ready, you see? (Group laughter)

And so, every book, every being, every experience is adding to this evolution of knowing. Do you see? Indeed you do. And so, where are you now?

We recommend to you, that you do that which excites you. If a book stimulates you, if you find that you cannot put it down, if you are feeling excited as you are reading it -- then read it. There is benefit for you within it. But as you are reading it, if it brings forth more negativity within you than it does positivity, (To Jerry, "That is another new word we have made up") then discard it, you see?

QUESTION: So as I get into a...book, if it is resistant to me, then leave it alone?

ABRAHAM: Put it away...We encourage you not to solicit opinions from others. They confuse. We encourage you to follow that which comes forth from you. If you ask for opinions, whose do you select, for they are all so very different, you see? TRUST YOURSELF. YOU MAY.

QUESTION: Something that puzzles me, a little bit: It seems like most of these metaphysical writings are pretty much...Am I off course in assuming that they are all on the same level with you, Abraham?

ABRAHAM: There are not two that are the same, for there are not two beings who have achieved the same level of consciousness or the same point of knowing. *Just because we are dead does not make us smart.*

And so, as you are hearing that which is not in harmony with who you are, discard it. Just as when you are interacting with your physical beings, there are those whose opinions seem more appropriate, because their life experience has brought them more knowing, you see? And so it is with those who are nonphysical. But you don't know the difference until you receive that which they offer. Do you see? For we all will tell you that we are the best. "We are the smartest of the nonphysical beings," you see?

QUESTION: Is it true that there is a plane beyond which you all are at this time, that you will go to?

ABRAHAM: There is no ending to growth, but there are not specific places that have been assigned. There is no ending, therefore there must be something beyond what is, you see.

QUESTION: I have an interest in what we will do after the "shift". I am not interested in food storage, and I'm not referring to this type of thing, but our personal life, our interaction with other people, and how we can be preparing for that?

ABRAHAM: It will be that which you create...It is too soon for you to begin projecting your vision of that, for there are too many unknowns for you, you see. And so, that is the reason you are asking this question. You are wanting Abraham to supply some of the unknowns, so that you may begin projecting into the future, and we are happy to do that.

We will tell you that you will be interacting with those that you are attracting, and it will be a time when you will be attracting more of those beings who are in harmony with your intent.

And so, it is a very good time for you to begin identifying what your intentions are now. In other words, if you are seeing yourself as one who is wanting to assist in healing, then you will attract those who are wanting to be healed. If you are seeing yourself as a being who is wanting to attract those who are as you are, who are teachers, or who are students and wanting to learn from teachers, then those are the beings that you will begin, even now, drawing toward you. If you see yourself as a savior, as one who will supply beans and rice for those who have not prepared, you will attract all of those who have made no preparation, you see, you will be overrun with those who are not prepared.

And so, it is our knowing that you will literally attract to you that which you are most wanting in that time, and there is not one experience that is better than the other. In other words, there is not that which is more noble or more appropriate. It all depends upon what you are wanting to experience.

We encourage you to stand back, from a broad perspective, and say, "I intend joyous creation and joyous harmony, joyous survival and joyous interaction with those who are in harmony with me."

Now, when we say, "in harmony," it means many things. *Harmony does not mean attracting someone who is exactly like you. Harmony means attracting those who will harmonize with you.* In other words, as you have talents in one area, harmony is attracting someone who has talents in another area. As you are adding what you have to offer, you will attract the others who will add the balance of that, you see. And so, as you are seeing yourself in this environment with everyone as participating, it will be a joyous time. That does not mean that we are envisioning for you a gathering of people all in one place where you are working together as in a commune type of thing. That is not what we are meaning -- unless that is what you are wanting, you see.

QUESTION: Thank you for that. I have one other question. This last couple of weeks I had some close friends visiting, and I can't get the point of Abraham across to them. All at once it seems like many people that I'm talking with are, I call them, just fat, dumb and happy. They don't have the least idea what is going on, and you want to be able to let them know, without them thinking you are a kook or something. Or is it better, maybe, not to say anything? I'm coming to that conclusion. Maybe it's better just to shut up and let them...But is that right?

ANOTHER'S QUESTION AND COMMENT: Doesn't it depend upon the situation and the time? Sometimes it is time to say something, and sometimes it isn't.

ANOTHER'S COMMENT: There is a time to stand up and say, and let people know, even if...we worry too much about how we're going to look...

ABRAHAM: Your great tool for teaching is your being. That which you are. *Your example is the greatest thing that you have*

to offer as you are wanting to influence thought in another.
Your words fall far short, and so do ours.

But we have no physical example, you see, and so we are stuck with words in this time. We promise you, that if we were physical beings, living in this time upon this earth, that you would see us joyously preparing for this time. And whenever anyone is around us saying, "What are you doing with all of this powdered milk?" we would say, "We are putting it aside for a time when it is not easy to find otherwise, for we are knowing that there is some changing that is about to occur, where there will be some severing of distribution routes."

"Well, what do you mean by that?"

"Well, it is our knowing that there are some physical changes that are about to occur. Every time we turn on the television we are seeing about it. There are earthquakes happening everywhere. Are you aware of the increase of frequency of earthquakes? You may not be aware because the scientists are not stating it, but I am aware because I have some inside sources. I am knowing those who are monitoring, and they are telling me that our earth is changing dramatically, and they have convinced me, and that is why I am doing this, you see."

And so, as you are making your preparation, others will say, "Not a bad idea." But as you speak the words, words have little meaning. There are many words that are abounding. There are so many words, you cannot hear them all. You cannot give your attention to all of them, you see.

And there is something more. There is a very basic tendency of those we see, who interact with you, to resist that which comes toward, too fast. As one senses that you are trying to make something happen, there is resistance, you see. And so, we encourage you to BE. Let them come to you with their wanting to understand, you see. For as you offer what is not asked, then there is often resistance, you see. And so, be a little obvious. Put your pile of food where it can not be not noticed, you see. As your friends are coming to see you, block the doorway with it, and say, "Oh, I am sorry that it is hard to get into this house, but I have this little pile of food that I am stashing away, for I am knowing I will be needing it," you see? Greet them with your face mask. (Group laughter) "I am practicing for when there will be dust in the air." (Group laughter) We are having fun with you, but you are understanding what we are saying.

COMMENT: I got the awareness across to them, because they had never heard anything about the shift. They didn't even know that there was a possibility of a shift. The awareness, the seed that I might have planted, could have been what they needed at that particular time.

ABRAHAM: Indeed. And that is our strongest point. If all your seed does is bring them to the point of saying, "I want to live on. I am just beginning this physical experience." Then that is quite enough.

Hear this: When you are ALLOWER, you will be able to allow them, even in their not allowing of you, you see. But there is more.

Your action follows your dominant intention. If your dominant intention is to provide a buffer zone for those that you are knowing, that they may have possibility of preparation -- then you will speak to everyone that you see. If your dominant intention is approval -- then you will speak to no one. (Group laughter) And so, it depends upon what your dominant intention is, and if you will bring it forth, consciously, more often, then it will be not so hard to make a decision.

We are understanding. Approval has been important for a very long time.

What more?

QUESTION: What if the media would start putting out things? Would that help?

ABRAHAM: There is a great deal being put out. Are you not aware of all of the information that is coming forth about the changing planet? There are many beings, who are in the know, who are offering forth much information, you see. That is why your proddings, your suggestions, your words, will not be so strange as you think.

Now hear this: Whenever you have stimulated thought, if you have stimulated it strongly enough -- positive or negative -- in other words, if you bring forth fear, or if you bring forth excited anticipation regarding this shift, in either case, all that enhances either one of those thoughts -- "joyous survival, or fear of dying in the earthquake" -- will be drawn to that being, and suddenly they will be reading a magazine, and they will turn to the page, and there will be something about it. They will turn on the television, there will be something about it, they will be standing in the grocery store, and there will be these people (pointing to Jerry and Esther) buying powdered milk and saying, "I am storing it." You see?

You must understand that that which is set forth in thought, will attract that which is like it. And so, it is quite enough for you to plant the seed.

JERRY: What if we didn't have a quake, a shift? What if people sell their homes and move into other areas...I mean, for us it doesn't make a difference because we just put away stuff we're going to eat anyway. The only thing I would be stuck with is face masks. And I could take up painting.

ABRAHAM: Let us talk about this, it is good. Let us paint the picture. "I have received information that the earth is about to change, and it has stimulated me to decide that I want joyous survival. And so, every thought that I set forth, from that point forward, is that of continuing this joyous life experience of interacting harmoniously with those who are in harmony with me -- and of having a wonderful life experience. And as I have set those thoughts forward, that is the life experience I will have.

And so, the worst thing that could happen, in terms of saving face, or preventing egg upon ones' face, the worst thing that could happen is that we may stimulate others to a zest for life that they have not had in many years -- and to a decision to take responsibility for doing something about it.

The best thing that could happen is that the earth will seek its balance, as it must do, to prevent destruction, and that everyone will be experiencing that which they are joyously preparing for. That everyone will have a holiday from that which they have created that has entangled them, and that there will be more deliberate creating, simultaneously, upon the face of the earth, than ever before in the history of man. Either way, we like it. What about you?

JERRY: Well, I'm having a great life.

ABRAHAM: Now, we say to you: Don't worry about it not happening. It is coming.

QUESTION: The thought I have there, though, is that if we think in this direction, so much, "that the shift is going to happen", could we, in fact, make it happen if it was, in fact, not going to happen?

ABRAHAM: You can not. Nor can you stop it from happening, in that light. Esther has said to us...Esther was very angry at us, for she waited a very long time to meet those who were older and wiser, and when they came forth (Abraham), they told her something she did not want to hear. She said, "Abraham, what happened to all of the promise of the good life? What is this business about destruction? I don't want to hear it!"

You have been co-creators in the creation of the planet upon which you are living, but you were part of that creation from a broader perspective, from a grander knowing, and as you created the earth, and all that surrounds it and participates with it, you have also set into motion this continual realignment.

Your earth is living, as you are, and just as your skin sheds and new skin grows, so does the "skin" of your earth. It is life. It is not death. It is not destruction. It is part of the process. And you accept it from your broader knowing.

And so, Esther is understanding that it is outside of her

creative license, and she said, "Well, I don't have to like it."
And we said to her, *"It is true, you don't have to like it -- and as
you think about that which you do not want, you will attract it
into your life experience. And so, it is good for you to begin
painting the picture of that which you do like, so that you will
begin drawing that."* And three days later she was ready to
speak with us again.
What more?

JERRY: Well, I still feel a little strange as I watch people in
San Diego, sell their homes...or leave their homes and busi-
nesses and move to places of safety, and so I was explaining
about some friends of ours who, as far as I knew, had no
money, they had nothing, but they understood that Tucson was
going to erupt, and their son came from the submarine service
and said, "Mom and Dad, I haven't spent any money in a couple
of years, and if you want to move to San Antonio, well, I'll sure
take care of it," and so, now they're living here in a beautiful
apartment and everything is so wonderful, here in San Antonio,
and so, I see their life as a lot better. I explained that they were
the people who could least afford it, and yet they were one of the
first to find a way, and the person I was explaining to said,
"Well, it is easy for them, because they had nothing to give up."

ABRAHAM: Hear this. For this will lead you back to where
we began this evening.
Solicit forth from those beings that you know and that
you love and that you see -- that which you want to see. In
other words, as you think of those beings, and as you see those
beings, see them as doing that which is in harmony with their
greater intent. Solicit forth from them, through your faith,
through your belief, their ability to reason and do that which is
appropriate for them. And allow them the choice, you see? As
you see them as hard headed beings, incapable of hearing anything, no matter how logical it is, and you see them stubbornly
staying there and dying, you may draw that forth from them.
But as you see them as beings who are creators of their own experience, lovers of life -- you will draw forth that from them,

you see? Indeed.

JERRY: Thank you.

COMMENT: If I might reiterate a statement that you made several months ago, that has helped me considerably with the thoughts of what could happen, "The transition from physical to nonphysical is not a bad experience."

ABRAHAM: Indeed, it is a glorious experience.

COMMENT: It has helped me a lot in understanding. Because that means, "Don't worry about who, or where, or what, or if, I am, because it is a joyous experience."

ABRAHAM: Indeed, it is.

QUESTION: There is one thing I'm not clear on.

ABRAHAM: Oh, it is good we have narrowed it down to only one thing.

COMMENT: At this moment, anyway. When you said, "See them as...whatever...and you will draw this from them?" I don't understand that.

ABRAHAM: You attract from one, that which you see. If you see a being as unwilling, they will be unwilling just to please you. If you see them as beautiful, they will be beautiful just to please you; if you see them as fat, they will be fat just to please you. If you see them as smart, they are smart, if you see them as dumb, they are dumb; if you see them as dead, they are dead.

QUESTION: Then you are creating it. Right?

ABRAHAM: You are not. You are using your power of influence. They have choice, you see.

JERRY: I've heard, through the years, how one baby sitter will say, "I can't stand that little brat," and another will say, "I don't understand that, he is always wonderful for me."

ABRAHAM: Indeed.

QUESTION: I understand that. I just didn't understand, since the creative process says that you cannot create in another's experience.

ABRAHAM: You cannot, for they have the choice. They make the conscious decision. Have you not seen it in yourself, that there are beings that when you are around them, you are at your very best, and there are beings that when you are around them, you are always at your very worst, and when it is over you say, "I do not know what is wrong with me." You are being swept up by the strong power of influence. And so, as you are wanting someone to be a certain way, see them in that way, and by your power of influence they *may* be that way for you.

COMMENT: So they create this, from your influence, by default.

ABRAHAM: If they are not understanding the process, and they usually are not.
It is all beginning to fit together for you. You are beginning to understand the power of thought and how you relate with one another, using it. You are beginning to understand the power of influence. You are beginning to understand your creative license, one with another. You are beginning to understand what freedom is, and very soon, you will have it all -- and you will be free.
It is with great appreciation that we interact with you, for we are seeing your discovery. You are of great value to us, for without your interaction, we would not be expressing clearly. Because of your willingness to hear and absorb, and chew upon it and then reflect back to us what you have received, because of that, we are evolving in our ability to communicate with physical

man, you see. And since that is our intent, there is great appreciation.

What you are witnessing here is that which we have promised to you earlier. The passageway is open, and that which you are experiencing is being received by ALL-THAT-IS, and ALL-THAT-IS, is liking it very much. Can you feel the emotion upon you? Indeed.

There is great love **here** for you! We are complete.

March 2, 1988

ABRAHAM: Good evening. We are extremely pleased that you are here. And now, as we are beginning, if you will take a moment and bring to your conscious mind that which you are most wanting to experience in this segment of your life experience that we are sharing here, it will be great value to you. (pause 20 seconds approximately)

While you would like a longer period of time, it is good practice to bring to your conscious mind, very quickly, as you are moving segment by segment, what is important, for often there is not a long segment in which to intend for the segment. Is that not right? What are you wanting to talk about?

QUESTION: I'd like for you to comment on "Parallel Realities and Probable Futures," and I was thinking specifically about the earth shift. We were discussing this yesterday...I realize that what you focus upon is what you bring into your experience, and I realize that the upcoming shift is something that has been set...a long time ago, but some of my friends were saying, "Well, if you focus on all the good things that are happening in the world right now, like the (agreement)...between the Soviet Union and us and Armenia, if you focus on all the good things, then that will bring more of that into your experience." What I'm wondering is, I sort of see it like the letter Y...If we become more aware of earthquakes that are happening and increasing, will that be the mainstay of our experience? Will we, sort of, enter into that, whole hog, or if we focus on the positive things that are happening, will we almost be unaware of the earth changes? I mean, will there be "Parallel Realities" that take place?

ABRAHAM: Indeed, there will be many realities, for there are not two of you who are anticipating precisely the same thing. And you are right. That which you are envisioning, that which you are thinking about, is that which you will attract. There are many beings who, as they are hearing about that which is to come, are stimulated to that which is fearful thought, and as they project that fearful thought forward, they begin attracting, even now, in this time, those sort of feared experiences, you see. But as you are seeing yourself as you are wanting to be, then that is what you will begin attracting to yourself.

Let us talk about this in the broader context, for it is something that may be applied to all creating that you are doing: As you are setting forth thought, you begin attracting the experience that you are thinking about, whether you want it or not -- that which you think about is that which you begin to attract, you see.

And so, as you are wanting to create a future that is in harmony with what you are wanting, then that future is that which you must think about. You must see yourself as prosperous, well fed, warm, surrounded by those beings who are in harmony with you. You must see yourself living that joyous experience that you are wanting. Particularly in this creation, where there are so many unknowns. There are so many things that you can't get your thoughts around, for it is difficult for you to anticipate what you will be doing for work. It is difficult for you to envision much of it, and as you try to get your logical thoughts around that which is unknown -- that is when you begin doing your most negative creating, you see, for there is so much that you do not understand, and when you feel yourself negatively creating...and how do you know it? There is negative emotion present. That is a very good time for you to back up from it, a bit, and look at it from the broader perspective.

Now hear this: As you are intending that which you are wanting from the broader view, in other words, something that is general, "I intend health. I intend happiness. I intend harmony..." you will begin attracting those sorts of experiences without ever putting the detail into it. But as you are clearer about the details that you are wanting, then begin inserting the details so that you are, in a more finely tuned way, drawing the specific creation to yourself that you are wanting. But in that process, if you find yourself struggling because there are un-knowns -- and because they are unknown, you are bringing forth negative thought and negative emotion -- then stop that, and back away from it again. And begin creating on a broader, more general scale.

     You see what we are saying? Know that you will be in a position to make those decisions then. And trust yourself. Say to yourself, "I am creator, and I am very wise, and in every day I will be able to make the appropriate decisions for that day." You see? And anything that causes you concern, release it, and go to your broader, more general creating of that which brings forth harmony. Clear enough?

QUESTION: Yes, and so if you totally focus on creating harmony and creating your future -- you know, just what we were saying -- just the way you want it, would you not even be aware of the earth changes?

ABRAHAM: It is possible. Not likely. But possible. You see, you are currently experiencing on many levels. In other words, you are currently a multidimensional being, participating in many dimensions, simultaneously, as you are here. And so, as you are focused here, and this is the dimension in which the earth changes are occurring, the you that is here will experience them. The other parts of you may or may not, depending upon how connected they are to you in this focused state, you see? And that may be what you are speaking about, but from the standpoint of those of you who sit here in this room now, in your physical, consciously focused state -- you will be aware.

     What more?

QUESTION; I have a daughter in California, who is there by

choice, but not by choice; she is married to a Marine. His choices, on a day to day basis, are very limited...

ABRAHAM: Indeed they are.

QUESTION: I have been unable to come up with the words to express to them how important I feel it is that they take a look at finding a way to be somewhere else. And I need help with the words?

ABRAHAM: Know this. That as you set forth thought that stimulates their thought, that their intent for survival is enough to set that creation in motion. Provided you have stimulated the thought enough to get them to chew upon it, you see.

None of us, no matter how powerful we are with words, and no matter how powerful our intent, may create within the experience of another, but as you stimulate their thought, they will begin attracting that which will give them their own intent. And so, speak from your heart. That which you have said to us, here, is most convincing, for it comes forth with love, and yet with allowing. You are not wanting to convince them to do something that is outside of their will, but it is very good for you to stimulate their thoughts so that they will identify what their will is, you see.

You see, as you are moving about, you have many intentions that are present, and a very dominant intention, especially in this case, is to stimulate the thought that they will choose that which will bring joyous survival, you see.

As you are interacting with others and you are very clear about your intent, the perfect words will come forth, you see, something such as, "It is clear to me that you are not in a safe place. How do you feel about the continuation of this physical experience?"

"Well of course we are wanting to continue. That is a very silly thing..." they will say to you.

COMMENT: That will be her exact answer. "Really Mother."

ABRAHAM: "Well, I was just wanting to stimulate your thought, for it is my knowing that you are wanting joyous survival, that I can release my worry..."

What more?

QUESTION: As far as influencing people. My mother-in-law's always had terribly high blood pressure, and I had to take her to the doctor for a check up, and we had to sit and wait in the doctor's office for a pretty good while, and as we were sitting there, she was telling me about her stiff neck, and I was telling her how to relax, and she said, "Well is that meditation?" which she resists, and I said, "No, that's just teaching you how to relax the muscles in your neck, and on down." Well, she was accepting it, and she felt really good about it, and I think she was sitting there trying to relax, and then the nurse came in and took her blood pressure, and it was lower than it had ever been. Can you explain?

ABRAHAM: It was your power of influence. It is the reason that you have chosen not to be in a dimension where you are alone. You have chosen to be surrounded by others, for you are wanting to influence others to the knowing that you are understanding, you see.

Let us talk about this interaction, for it is a very important topic. You are together with one another, involved in agreements, involved in relationships much of your life experience. And yet, most of you do not understand how it is that you do influence one another and just what this relationship is all about. What is the broader reason for it, you see. Of course, it is because it brings you joy. As you interact with one another, there is enhancement of all that is wonderful. But there is something more, for what you are wanting to understand, perhaps more than anything that you are wanting to understand in this physical life experience, is that you are wanting to become ALLOWERS. Now, when we are saying, "allowers," we are meaning that you are wanting to be as you are and reach the state where you are willing to allow others to be as they are wanting to be -- even if they are not wanting to allow you to be as you are.

Now, we have talked a great deal about the Creative Process, and we will talk about it more tonight, for we are wanting you to understand how it is that you get what you get in your life experience. Most of you do not understand it. Most beings who are physical are doing most of their creating by default. They set forth thoughts; they attract creation; they do not understand that they have done it, and so they blame someone else.

And so, as you understand that you are the creator of that which you receive, that nothing comes into your experience without your invitation, and that you invite through your thought, then you have total freedom, for no matter how terrible the actions of another are, and no matter how close they are to you, you do not fear them -- because you understand that they will not be part of your experience unless you invite them through thought.

Now, as you are understanding that, then you are willing to allow them to be, you see, for now they are no threat to you. There is no more need for walls, or wars. No more do you need to gather together in camps for power, for you understand that you are individually strong. Individually strong enough to be or have or do whatever you are wanting, no matter what is happening around you, you see.

Now, as you understand that as you set forth thought, you literally attract the experience from the universe...then you understand how it is that you solicit response from your fellow beings, you see.

Now hear this: Even your greatest enemy has more points of harmony with you than disharmony, but the reason they are your enemy is because you focus upon that which you do not like -- and anything that you focus upon, you attract. And so, as you are looking at this being who you are not wanting to be with very much -- you are not liking, for he is your enemy -- you attract more of that which you do not want, you see.

What we are saying to you is that you may have wonderful relationships even with those beings that currently you cannot imagine it -- if you would focus upon your points of harmony, and there are many.

Now, what are you wanting to talk about?

COMMENT: In carrying the Creative Process further, I have some questions about it specifically. It comes to me, that the *details* of getting where we want to be, are where we may miscreate.

ABRAHAM: Absolutely.

QUESTION: OK. That is really what I was wondering. Because, we say, "I want to triple my income," or something like that, and, immediately, I think, "How can I do that?" And that's what we have to do away with, the specifics on how to get from here to there?

ABRAHAM: We are not wanting you to do away with it. Now hear this. This is the Creative Process: Want it and allow it -- and it is. If you will want it and then allow it, it will be.

Now there are many things that you are wanting, and usually there is not a lot of suppressing of the wanting. We will talk about that, but it is the "allowing" part that is, for the most part, a hindrance for you -- and the allowing includes ALL of your beliefs. If you do not believe that you should, or can, then you usually will not, you see? Now, you are saying, "I am wanting a car." Until you get very specific about it, you may not get very excited about it, and when you understand that specifics bring forth excitement, then you understand the value of the specifics. For the more you are able to visualize it, the more excited you will be, and your emotion empowers your creation, you see.

If you want something very much, it is coming to you very fast, and if you fear something very much, it is coming to you very fast. And so, you say, "I want a new car." It is on its way. But as you get more specific, and more excited, then it is on its way to you more quickly.

Now, let us say you are driving down the street. You have already made your statement in that day, "I am wanting a new red car. I want it to be a car of this year, and the color red, and I am wanting it to have all of these things...." And as you are driving down the freeway, you look out of your window and there it is! And as you see it you get excited. You slow down so that you can be with it longer. And the more you look at it, the happier you get. You speed up, and you look at it in your mirror, and you slow down, and you look at it from behind. (Group laughter) You say, "It is a wonderful vehicle. I have never seen it moving before. Oh, I can smell it! I can feel myself in that car! I will have it, it is on its way!" And this emotion that you are feeling is bringing it to you more quickly.

However, if you look over, and you see it, and it makes you grouchy because you have wanted it for so long and you do not have it yet, now you are pushing it away. Or if you say, "His father probably bought it for him, and I have to earn mine." (Group laughter) You are pushing it farther away. If the emotion that you feel as you see that automobile is negative rather than positive, or not feeling good instead of feeling good, you are pushing it away. The way you feel helps you to know whether you are bringing it or pushing it.

Now, if you cannot bring yourself to the point of getting excited, then it is better not to think about it at all, and go back to your broader perspective of, "I am wanting a new car." Very often, as you get caught up in the specifics of your creating, you miscreate. Now this is why:

When you are in the specifics, you are using your logical mechanism, and your logic can only give you what it knows from your experience. And so, if you have never had this wondrous vehicle, and you are counting upon your logic, your logic will say, "You can't have it -- for you have never had it." Do you understand?

QUESTION: Like if you can't afford it?

ABRAHAM: Oh, there are one hundred or more reasons: "The insurance will be more. Red cars get more tickets...." There are many reasons that you will uncreate this car, you see.

QUESTION: OK. Then I guess what I'm thinking about, more specifically, is (if we're wanting to use a car as an example) and say that I know that I can have that car because I can see that if I earned this amount of money, I will be able to afford that car...that's the specifics that I'm talking about.

ABRAHAM: That is the bridge. That is the bridge from the negative thought and negative emotion to the positive thought and positive emotion.

QUESTION: Except, but what if you don't have enough money to have the car?

ABRAHAM: Then your negative emotion will remain, and you will continue to push the car away.

QUESTION: I see, but if I want something, so very much, like say a beautiful home, and I don't see it within my means to buy a new home, but I still want it, and can feel excited about it, am I still creating it?

ABRAHAM: In the moment that you are excited about it, you are. In the moment that you are worried about it and thinking you cannot afford it, you are pushing it away. And that is the way most of your creations are. They are floating around in limbo out here somewhere. Created, just not coming into your experience, because you attract them and push them, attract them and push, attract them and push them, you see.
    And the key is to monitor the way that you feel, and whenever you feel negative emotion, stop doing whatever you're doing. Stop thinking, speaking or acting; stop doing whatever it is that has brought forth that negative emotion.
    Now that doesn't mean you have to fix the thought. That doesn't mean you have to convince yourself you can afford it. It means you have to stop thinking that you can't afford it -- by thinking of something else.

COMMENT: Distraction.

ABRAHAM: Distraction.
    Now hear this: Let us begin again for the benefit of those who have not heard. We will speak very quickly this pro-

cess...Want it and allow it and it is. Make a statement "I intend." "Intend" is more powerful than "want," for intend includes the expectation *and* the wanting. "I intend," and whatever it is, "for these reasons." Write the reasons that came from you. Not the reasons that someone wants you to want it. Write the reasons that you want it. There is power in *your* wanting. There is no power in someone else's wanting for you. Until *you* are wanting it, it is not powerful for *you*. On the other side of your paper write all of the reasons that you know it will be. That enhances the belief, or the allowing, part of the equation. Consider it done. Fold your paper, put it in your pocket, and say "That was easy. What is next?" If you will not think about it in negative terms again, it will be yours. And if you will think about it in positive terms, very often, it will be yours very quickly.

Now, you are moving through your day. As long as you are feeling only positive emotion, or only no emotion, it is on its way to you, but in the moment you are feeling negative emotion about that subject, you are pushing it away. Now, if you will say, "I am feeling negative emotion; what do I want?" regarding any subject, distracting yourself in any way, so that you stop that miscreating, that is very good. You will stop the miscreating. However, that thought may come up again and again and again, you see. So if you will deal with it by saying, "What thought brought forth this feeling?" And it will take you a moment. It may take a few moments to isolate the thought, for as you are aware, there are many thoughts that happen all at once, and so, if you are conscious of your negative emotion, it may be a few moments after it began, you see, for you may not be aware of it instantly, and so, as you recognize that you have negative emotion, and you say, "What thought has brought this forth? Well, I was thinking about that, and I was thinking about that, and I was thinking about that, and then that led to that, and that led to that..." When you come upon the thought that is the culprit, it will be as if you have touched a sore spot, for your negative emotion will read louder and clearer for just that moment, and you will say, "Ah ha, this is the thought. I was remembering my mother's discouraging words as I expressed my desire for this beautiful car. What do I want? I want the car.

Not having the car, does not necessarily mean that I will please her, for there are many things that she wants for me, or does not want for me, that I do not agree with. I am the creator of my experience. She is the creator of her experience. I want this beautiful car, and I know that I will have it soon." As you bring yourself from this negative thought and negative emotion, to this positive thought and positive emotion, once you have made that bridge, you have changed your belief.

You see, a belief is a creation, and a creation is never complete. You mold your belief, or your creation of thought, which is a belief -- by applying new thought to it, and once you have done that, it will no longer hinder you, for now you have changed it. But if you use the route of distraction, never bothering to bridge and change the thought, then it will continue to come up to haunt you.

Now, your point is a very good one. As you are moving through your day, and you are suddenly filled with negative emotion, and you cannot identify a thought that explains it, then there is very likely something that is within your experience, some sort of wanting. For example: You are walking through a dark parking lot. And you have been thinking about the happy movie that you just saw, or about the experience you are about to have, and you are moving along, very happily, and suddenly you are filled with intense stress, negative emotion, fear...There may very well be something that your Inner Being is sensing, that you are not consciously aware of. Respond to the fear by moving very quickly, or at least by looking around and making sure, you see. But if you are walking through the dark parking lot, and you are finding yourself filled with fear, but you remember that you just saw "Chain Saw Massacre" at the theater, and it is what your thoughts are filled with, then understand that it is very likely that you have created the thought which has brought forth the fear, do you understand?

Your emotions are communication from your Inner Being. They are not like your nose or your toe. They are communication from the inner world in which your Inner Being, which is a very real part of you, exists. And so, as you are sensitive to those emotions, you have the advantage of much knowing that you may not consciously be aware of. *Your Inner Being is*

watching over you from a broader standpoint, and your Inner Being is understanding ALL of the intentions that you hold, you see.
Now, as you are finding yourself filled with anxiety, there is reason for it. And it is a good thing to spend some time sorting it out to see if you cannot identify what thought is present when the anxiety comes forth. We will talk more about that. It is good.

QUESTION: Along those same lines, every time that I visit with my mother, I get all these emotions. But yet I can't, I don't want to, stop visiting my mother, you know, and I'm trying to deal with that, because, everything she says is so negative, and everything is so fatalistic, and I want to guard myself from all that negativity, but I want some words, that, maybe, will help me, at least, be able to deal with those feelings?

ABRAHAM: We've talked about this before, for it is something that you are struggling with. You see, your action always follows your dominant intention.
As your dominant intention is to think only upon that which you are wanting, but you are continually visiting with this one who influences your thought in the direction of what is not wanted, you must understand that there is another intention that is dominant other than your wanting not to speak of that which is not what you are wanting. Your dominant intention is to please your mother. Your dominant intention is that of harmony, and so, you are continually following through with that, unable to distract yourself as you are interacting.
Perhaps the way we began this evening will be of value to you: As you are recognizing that your mother has many more points of harmony than disharmony, and you insist upon focusing only upon those -- you will have less pain.
Now hear this: *As you are understanding that that which you are most wanting to understand is to be allower, and that being allower will bring you absolute freedom, then you will be able to allow her, even in her not allowing of you.* As she is speaking of those things which you are not wanting, disregard them. That is not really the problem. The warning bells ring

loudest when she is concerned about what you are doing. You are not doing that which she thinks you should do. But when you are able to say, "It is all right that you feel that way. I understand," and really mean it, then you will be free of the negative emotion that comes forth under these conditions, you see.

It is easiest to remove yourself physically, and if you did not have the intent of wanting family harmony, she would have been gone from your life long ago, you see, but as you have this other intention, you are putting yourself in a position where you must consciously make the decision that you will not participate in that which brings forth negative emotion. Now that does not mean that you can bandage her mouth shut. For that is outside of your creative license, but you can bandage your own ears shut, you see. You can stop hearing that which upsets you -- even though you hear the words -- when you are willing to say, "It is all right. I hear what you say, but this is what I know to be." Then those feelings will not be so intense within you -- and you will be free.

FREEDOM COMES WHEN YOU ARE ABLE TO BE AS YOU ARE AND TO ALLOW OTHERS TO BE AS THEY ARE!

You are inviting her with your thought. You have invited her into your experience with your thought, indeed, but you even invite that which hurts you with your thought. Even as we are talking about it now, you are feeling the negative emotion, and she is not even here. It is the thought, you see. (She laughs)

What more?

QUESTION: Abraham, I have lots of relatives in a dangerous area, and I'm very concerned about them...Will there be time for them to get out? Will there be enough time, from the first warning tremor, so that they can be safe?

ABRAHAM: In most places that which will occur will occur very rapidly. There is a broader issue here. Let us talk about it: *You must understand that you are the creator of your experience and everyone else is creator of theirs.* And as you have stimulated their thought with what you are knowing, you must release them to go about their creating around it, you see. And you must be willing to allow them to make those choices.

What we are talking about, here, is not an easy thing to consciously get your thoughts around, for as we said earlier: Your conscious logical mind wants to talk about that which it has experience for, or if you have not had personal experience, it at least wants written documentation by those who are "in the know," you see. And so, as we are talking about a subject where there is not written documentation, for that which has occurred before has not allowed the survival of written documentation, now you are in a position where you must make your decisions about what you will do based on your faith. Based on your belief. There is not conscious, physical fact for you to hang your hat on. This time you must decide what you are wanting without someone else's influence, you see.

Now, as you are letting those beings know that you are having a strong sensing, you will begin to hear from them things that will surprise you. Esther and her mate have just been in San Diego, and as they were going to San Diego, Esther said, "Abraham, I am not very happy about this, for it is quite different to visit with *these* beings. It is different than saying, "Store some food and some masks for your nose." These beings must make a decision to stay where they are and die, or remove themselves to a place that is safe. It is a much bigger decision here. I am not sure I am up to it"

And we said to her, *"Esther, it has nothing to do with you. You are but stimulator of thought. They are the creator of their experience. You must not assume responsibility for their decisions."* And so, we began visiting with them, one at a time, and one after the other said, "Abraham, I am sensing something. Can you tell me what it is?" Or they said, "Abraham, our children are dreaming that the ocean is coming. What does this mean?" You see, once you have stimulated the thought, they will be aware of that which they currently have not been aware of. They will turn on the television, and they will see the geologists speaking of the increased activity all over the world. They will pick up a paper, and they will see that there are earthquakes occurring in places that are not usual. They will begin to notice the weather changes. They will stand in the grocery store next to this one who is buying extra food, and she will say to them, "I am putting it away, for I am aware that there are earth changes that are occurring."

You see, as you stimulate the thought, those beings who are wanting joyous survival, and there are many who do, will begin drawing life experience that will confirm to them and help them make their decision about what they will do. If you convince them against their will, you are assuming responsibility, and they will come back to you later with blame.

If you take the responsibility to convince someone of something against their will, and they do it just to please you, without it being a choice of their own, they will never accept the outcome of it, good or bad, they will always hold you responsible. Do you understand? Now if you are wanting that sort of responsibility, then twist arms everywhere you go, regarding *everything,* and if you are not, then use your power of example. That is your greatest power of influence.

Be who you are, and speak what you know, and let everyone else *decide.* You will find comfort in that.

QUESTION: Abraham, don't you think that everybody is captain of their own ship and master of their own fate? If our loved ones die, it's because they chose to, and because they will return.

ABRAHAM: Indeed. They are choosing. Some deliberately, and many by default, and in either case, it is a joyous transition. Not something to worry about.

COMMENT: Yes, you really can't get caught up in, "How can I save my child," because that child is an entity unto itself, now, as we are all entities, and it should come into the situation...."

COMMENT: Sadness is really a selfish thing.

ABRAHAM: Sadness is a negative emotion coming forth from Inner Being, saying to you, "In this moment, that which you are thinking is not part of your intent," you see?

You are uplifters, and you are wanting to interact to uplift, you see, and that is very good.

As you experience joy, and uplift others to joy, your joy is compounded, you see? And so, that is why you are wanting this.

As teacher, you will come to understand that you can but offer, and it is up to the others to receive, and it is the law of it, you see. You cannot do it all for them. It is not what they intended as they came to physical form, and it is not what they intend in the nonphysical dimension. Every being is individual creator, wanting that, you see?

What more?

QUESTION: Abraham, I live very close to the river. Can I assume that this is not a safe place to be?

ABRAHAM: Let us talk about this, for we are upon a subject that could take from here until forever, as we discuss every place that there is. And so, what we are going to do, now, is give you an opportunity to have this knowing yourself:

You are understanding that you are receivers of communication from your Inner Beings, are you not? If you have experienced emotion, positive or negative, you are receivers. There is not an exception. In this room or in any other.

Now, we are wanting each of you to understand your own power of receiving. You have the ability, all of you, to receive in this way if you are wanting it, and many of you are, but you are not trusting. It is easier to hear the words from another than to trust those that come through yourself, and it is all right, but what we are wanting you to do is to begin, now, the process of trusting *yourselves*. Now here it is:

Each of you choose a spot. Whatever you are wanting. Visualize yourself sitting in the middle of the home that you now live in, and this is the statement that we are setting forth: We are asking the Inner Being, of each being who is here with us, to bring forth emotion that will confirm the safety of the individual spot that you are thinking about. With the feeling of positive emotion meaning safe, the feeling of negative emotion meaning not safe.

Now, you are understanding that there are only two emotions. One feels good and one does not. Whether you are calling it guilt or loneliness or fear or hatred or anger, it all feels like a raw donut in your stomach.

And now, we will be quiet for a moment, while each of you sense from your Inner Being as to the safety of the location you are envisioning.

ABRAHAM: ....you are receiving nodding. (many indicating negative feelings) Indeed, now we will not continue in this vein, for we are not wanting to attract negative emotion, unnecessarily, but we are wanting you to understand that you may confirm the comparative safety of any place, you see? In fact, you may receive answers regarding anything -- the appropriateness or inappropriateness of -- through this "yes" or "no" sort of technique. *And as you do it more and more, you will begin to trust yourselves more and more, and as you trust yourselves more and more, you will have more clear conscious guidance.*

If you will see your emotion as an absolute guidance system, as the beam that brings the airplane in, you will find that you will not need to be off of your track at all.

QUESTION: Why use a "yes" and "no" system when you can use something like a Ouija or something of that nature?

ABRAHAM: As you are blended -- this conscious physical being that is sitting there, and the Inner Being that is within you -- then you may receive many means of communication. You may speak as Esther is speaking, you see, or use a board.

The reason that we are not ordinarily recommending the use of the board is because it is known to be a game, and there are many frivolous beings in the nonphysical dimension who also understand that it is a game, you see. And so, there is a lot of fun had with it if you are not understanding clearly what you are wanting.

Your Inner Being will not play a game with you upon something that is serious, but there are frivolous beings, you see?

COMMENT: They do constantly lie at times.

ABRAHAM: Just because we're dead doesn't mean we're smart. And it doesn't mean we're in harmony with you, either, you see? And so it is good for you to find a direct path to that which will not tease you.

COMMENT: No practical jokes.

ABRAHAM: Indeed.

QUESTION: Are there such things...I heard this, the other day -- as pixies and elves and fairies and all that, that are supposed to be channeling too, as well as animals?

ABRAHAM: You must understand that that which is "channeled," as you say, that which is received through thought through the nonphysical dimension, is created into whatever it is wanted to be, or whatever it is expected to be, by the being who is receiving.

Abraham is not something that you could describe in your physical terms. We are energy. We are thought. Now, the way that Abraham is manifest, here, because of Esther's expectation and from what she is knowing from Abraham -- is a very wise and caring, loving teacher. But, if her expectations were that it were a pixie, it is possible that you may be receiving something a bit more pixie-like. (Group laughter) The expectation of the receiver is that which creates.

You see, you are part of life experience, which is literally that which you have been hearing about. It is the time of AWAKENING. You will be physical beings upon the earth at the great time of awakening that has been written about, only it will not be as many of you have expected it to be.

The awakening will occur within *you,* and what it is is the blending of your conscious physical being with your Inner Being, you see. It is your saying, "I recognize that I am more than I see. And I am wanting the enhancement of this physical experience by the greater knowing that comes forth from within."

194

Now, not so very long ago, physical man upon the earth
-- when we say, "not so very long ago," we are meaning a few
hundred thousand years -- man upon the earth was not recognizing that there was anything that he could not see, touch or
smell.

And so, there was no looking to the heavens for guidance. And then, in time, there were those who believed that
there were gods. There was the god of this and the god of that.
Not one god, many gods. And then -- we are jumping very
large jumps -- but then you began to recognize that there *was*
something that was divine, not so very long ago in your evolution. There were those beings in physical form who thought that
as thoughts came through, it was in the form of a dead relative,
always expressing about the "rabbits foot," or something, so
that you would know that it was, indeed, coming from the other
side, you see. And then you began to believe that there was
spiritual guidance, and you began to call them "spiritual guides."
"One was assigned to each of you," you see, and if you sought
long enough, you would find that one.

*And now, what we are wanting you to understand, is
that each of you has access to Infinite Intelligence, and that as
you allow the opening of the passageway, within your very being, that this physical experience, this conscious physical experience in which you are currently focused, will be enhanced.*

*We are not wanting to distract you from the physical life
in which you live, to put you into the clouds, or focus you in
another dimension. We are wanting you to experience that
which you have intended, with the enhancement of the knowing
that comes forth from within, you see. And that is accomplished
by the opening of the passageway.*

QUESTION: This past weekend I experienced my first channeling, with two different entities, and I would like to know if
you could help me with doing some more of it, learning to release the control I maintain. Everyone seems to think that I have
this control or whatever it is. Could you give me some advice?

ABRAHAM: As with anything that is new, you will become
more comfortable with it as you are doing it longer.

Make no comparison about that which you have experienced here, with Esther, for your experience is your own. It is very good. Do more of it, and as you sit, let your intent be, "I intend to speak clearly."

COMMENT: I don't know which one I would get, if it's either of these two, I think they were just, kind of, experimenting during that time.

ABRAHAM: Ask to speak to those who come forth from where your Inner Being is. That is always best. Ask to speak with those of your "Family", you see.

QUESTION: Is there some control that I need to learn, to release?

ABRAHAM: It is a matter of quieting your mind and stating your intent clearly, and as you are receiving it, you will get better and better at it.
     You see, the tendency is to come here and hear this one (Esther) one who has spoken for us for thousands of hours. If you could have been here at the beginning, you would have seen something that is quite different. There would be a very long question, beautiful in words, and Abraham would say, "That is correct." And then there would be another very eloquent and long question, and then Abraham would say, "It is not exactly like that." And then there would be another very long question, you see, and it was not that Esther was not receiving, it was that she was not trusting all that she was receiving, and so she would speak that which she did trust, you see? And so, as you are speaking more and more, you will trust more and more. You will become more comfortable with that which comes forth. Are you understanding what brings this possibility?

COMMENT: Allowing.

ABRAHAM: Indeed. You are physical beings who are not only the flesh and blood that has been created here in the physical dimension, but you have energy surging through you that comes from the inner dimension, and that energy surges through you, all of you -- it is what makes the difference between whether you are dead or alive -- and so, as this energy surges through you, you say, "I am alive. And everyone else must feel alive in the same way that I feel alive," although you don't really know that.

And so, what is necessary is that that energy, that you are not used to, must blend with the energy that is within you. That is the blending. That is the opening that we are speaking about, and that is why you feel movement, tingling, twitches. It is not that there is a passageway that is chopped out. It is that the energy is aligned, you see. And so, the more that you are allowing it, the more time you are spending doing it, the more comfortable it becomes, you see.

QUESTION: Should I speak out when there is no one else to hear it. When I am just meditating by myself?

ABRAHAM: Oh, indeed. The more the better. The more you are receiving, the more you will trust.

QUESTION: Should I speak my questions out loud?

ABRAHAM: Indeed. Let us talk about the process for the opening of this passageway -- for the benefit of those who are wanting it. Do not worry, if you are not wanting it, you will not get it. It is not something that will be thrust upon you if it is not something that you are wanting.

Now, as with all creation, want it and *allow* it -- and it is. Want it and allow it -- and it is. And so, as you are wanting the opening of the passageway, you have done most of it.

The allowing is what we are offering the process of meditation for. When we use the label, "meditation," what we are meaning is this: Setting a time aside in your physical world that you may quiet the physical so you may sense the inner. And the process is just sitting quietly and being.

Now you say, "We are always being. How can we not be?" Well, when we say "be," we mean, don't try to make anything else happen. Sit quietly, and don't think of anything. Well, as soon as we say, "Don't think of anything," you think of not thinking of anything, but what you must do is quiet your mind -- and a good way is to focus upon something that does not require much conscious thought. Something such as your breathing. As you will allow the air to go out and come in, and you will be aware of it, and you will let your thoughts drift toward that, very soon, perhaps even in the first sitting, you will find yourself with a sort of tingling sensation. You will find yourself, perhaps, even numb. As you are feeling that sensation of numbing, know that it is a signal to you, from your Inner Being, that you have achieved the quieting of the physical so that you may now sense the inner. And, as you are upon that plateau of numbness, as you think a thought, it will go away, as you release the thought and quiet your mind, it (the numbness) will come back, and as you are able to move up and down upon this, soon you will get very good at being at that place, and once you are consistently achieving that, you are in the state of allowing.

Now, as you are in the state of allowing, your work is done. Your Inner Being will do the rest.

And as you are feeling some tingling here and a sensation there, those sensations are an indication to you that your Inner Being is working upon the opening of your passageway, or aligning your energies. And when you receive movement, you are open. What do you think about that?

Now, once you are open, it is not necessary that you sit in a state of meditation to receive. Once you are open, you may receive, any time you are wanting, by setting forth the intent, "I intend to receive," you see?

The meditation is a process for opening the passageway. Beyond that, we are not seeing it as important, unless you are using it for other things, you see.

There are many intentions for the meditation. Some of you meditate, which is the process of quieting the physical so that you may sense the inner, because you are tired of the physical. You are wanting relief from it. You are wanting rest from it, and that is good, but do not assume that you must be in a state of meditation to receive. Esther is not in a state of meditation.

She has opened her passageway through the state of meditation, and she receives whenever she chooses, do you see? And you may, as well.

QUESTION: What keeps another entity, other than you, from taking over Esther during that time?

ABRAHAM: Her clear intent. She is knowing that she is wanting to receive from those from which she has come. She is wanting to receive from her Family. And once she has made contact with her Family, the others will not bother her.

You see, until you have made contact with the one from which you have come, then you are sort of fair game to everyone. Particularly, if you have made contact otherwise. But once you have made contact with the Family from which you have come, the others say, "Agreed, it is done." As Esther is here moving into the segment of her day where she is intending to receive, if she is not saying, "I am wanting to speak with Abraham, or with those from whom I have come," if she says, "Universe I am here, speak to me. Anybody out there. I'll take any of you who is nearest," she may receive something that is not in harmony with who she is, you see. And so, we do not recommend that. We recommend that you say, "I am wanting, through this opening, to receive that from which I have come." And once you do that, the others will not bother you.

QUESTION: OK. You came to her as one?

ABRAHAM: We did, for that was her expectation. She did not understand who we were then. She was saying, "I am wanting to know my spiritual guide." And the day we came to her we said, "I am Abraham. I am your spiritual guide."

QUESTION: What if they come to you in separate personalities? Separate beings, and thoughts. How do you bring them together?

ABRAHAM: By intending it. By understanding it. You see...

QUESTION: And if they refuse?

ABRAHAM: Then tell them you will have no more of it. ✗
That you are the keeper of your being, that you are the creator of *True*
that which you experience, and it is done.

Those who are in harmony with you will never refuse
what you are intending, you see. Those who are not in harmony, release them.

Do not worry. You see, there is great worry about
"possession." It was Esther's greatest fear, it is why it took us
so long to get together, you see.

QUESTION: Won't it create an imbalance if they were meant
to have this assortment of people together?

ABRAHAM: *There is nothing that was meant to be. You are
creator of your experience here,* you see. You are intending to
find that blending with your Inner Being.

Now hear this; it will help you a great deal; for all of you
who are seeking communication with the inner dimension, this
will be very important to you:

Your expectation -- hear this -- your allowing, your beliefs, play a very big role in that which you receive...

If you are expecting communication in some (particular) *True*
way, you will not allow it in any other way. And because your
Inner Being is wanting the communication, it will be whatever
you expect it to be, in the beginning, so that you may have the
experience, you see? And then, bit by bit, you are given information that helps you to understand the broader story.

When Abraham met Esther, Esther saw Abraham as one
being. One guide. One soul assigned to her. And she was so
happy that there was this guide that could tell her what to do.
*Then she discovered that Abraham did not intend to tell her what
to do. Abraham is teacher, wanting to offer guidance, but Esther must decide what she is wanting to do, for Esther is creator
of her experience,* you see.

And so, soon she stopped saying, "Abraham should I eat
this or should I not, should I go right or should I go left." Soon

she understood that Abraham would give her principles by which she could make decisions, you see, and so, bit by bit, the relationship between Esther and Abraham has evolved to what you see it today -- and it is not finished yet. There will be much more that is understood as time goes by, you see.

What we are wanting you to do is to create the experience that you choose, and we will tell you what your Inner Being intended. Now hear this:

All of you who are in physical bodies upon the earth, at this time, have come forth from an Inner Being. An Inner Being who made the decision, "I want to be physical in this time." You have specifically chosen this time upon planet earth, for you are aware of the increase in the creative energy that would allow you, not only more interaction with the inner dimension, but faster creativity. You, very much, wanted to be here, and your Inner Being, the you of you....as we break you into parts, we talk about your Inner Being and your physical being, we fragment you, but our intent is to blend you. To help you to find harmony. To help you to see that you are one great and wondrous being -- and it is with that being that you seek this contact.

Do not see yourself as an instrument that must speak with anything that is wanting to talk. You may be the deliberate creator of that, and we encourage you to ask for your Inner Being, your higher self, your soul, your GOD, whatever you are calling it. Ask for that which you want to experience, and that is what you will receive, do you see?

Now where have we left you? Are you wanting to speak?

QUESTION: Would you allow Esther to use the board?

ABRAHAM: We are not the allowers for Esther. She is the chooser of her experience, you see.

QUESTION: Does she choose to use the board?

ABRAHAM: She has. She would not now, for she had the worst experience of her lifetime upon it. It was two weeks be fore she would talk to us again. What more?

COMMENT: The last time I was here, we were asking about the time narrowed down with the earth shift, and you were telling us early summer, which is June.

ABRAHAM: And now we tell you to receive it yourself. (Group laughs.)

QUESTION: And then later you said, "Have your preparations done by early May, and so, then I was wondering if the big jolt was coming in June but was going to get started in May, or what exactly...?

ABRAHAM: *What we are saying to you is that we don't know when it will be.* We are knowing that it is near, and we are also knowing that it is much better to be ready for it in May, and have it occur in June, than to be ready for it in June, and have it occur in May, and so the sooner you make preparation the happier you will be, you see.

It is our knowing that it will be very soon, but soon in terms of our time is not easy for you to understand. We are sensing -- through those who are upon your earth, and we have many connections that are difficult to explain -- that your earth is changing very rapidly, and as this is not our first earth shift, we believe that our calculations are rather accurate. *You may sense through your inner knowing, as it draws nearer, using the method that we have offered here earlier.*

QUESTION: Regarding guilt, I was thinking of that in reference to someone who murders someone, or something like that. Their thought would be of guilt, because they'd done that?

ABRAHAM: It depends upon the state of their being, you see. The Inner Being, that you come forth into this physical dimension from, has great knowing. You have had much life experience. And so, as you are experiencing life, and you are seeing things that others are doing that you are not feeling very good about, as you are seeing them kill one another, and it makes you feel bad, understand that the reason that you have this keen knowing is because you have had that experience.

Everyone has killed someone, in one lifetime or another - - and has been killed. That is how you know how you feel about it, you see. And so, those emotions come forth from that greater knowing, and that is the reason that there are some things...that are simply not in harmony with who you are.

As someone is wanting to suppress your freedom, great negative emotion comes forth, for freedom is inherent to your very being, you see. And so, there are cases when a feeling of negativity would come forth, that you could call guilt, as you are about to do something that your Inner Being is very sure you are not really wanting to participate in at this level of development, you see. And it is responding to the thought. You will get that feeling even as you are *thinking* about that which you might want to do, you see what we are saying?

QUESTION: Are there as many different Inner Beings as there are physical beings on earth, or does each physical being have a unique Inner Being, is what I'm trying to say, or is one Inner Being expressing in a number of physical beings simultaneously?

ABRAHAM: All of that. (Group laughter) There are some Inner Beings who are physically only focused in one. There are some Inner Beings who are focused in more. There is some of all of it. It is a different situation depending upon the intent of the Inner Being.

QUESTION: Then that goes on to the next idea. Are we created from one source? Are we really one?

ABRAHAM: You are.

QUESTION: All of us? Everything?

ABRAHAM: Indeed. Absolutely.

QUESTION: Separated into Families by intention?

QUESTION: And that's why we can have Families of different intentions that are not in harmony with each other?

ABRAHAM: That is correct.

QUESTION: If Esther has the power to keep out other entities when she has the "pipe" open, if she can keep out other entities and only allow the one in that she wants, then why can't Esther -- or Esther and a group of people who think along the same lines -- prevent the shift from occurring by just willing it not to occur? It seems like the first thing is a very powerful happening.

ABRAHAM: It is. It is an excellent question and perhaps the first question that Esther set forth to us once she was clear in understanding that the shift was something that was occurring. She said to us, "Abraham, you have convinced me that I am invincible, and so, Abraham, I tell you this: I will not have it. And so, you do whatever you need to do, but I want it stopped." And we said to her, "Good. Are there others who feel the same way?" "Indeed."

We said, "Gather your friends together, and while you are at it, intend that the sun will not come up in the morning, and intend that winter will not come in this year, for, you see, you have set forth the creation of this earth, and you are part of it, you are all co-creators of the creation of your earth, but you set it forth at a level of creation that is beyond that which you are currently focused within here as you are upon the earth, and it is by your agreement, that you are here in this capacity, you see."

The earth, and all that surrounds it, was set into motion by a great and powerful wanting, and part of that wanting said, "We want this earth to exist for a very long time."

It is a living earth. It is living, as everything upon it is living. And as it is living, it is growing, and just as you are growing new skin, so is this earth growing new "skin". And as it is evolving and changing, it is continually seeking its balance. Your Inner Being understands that if the earth does not find its balance, that it will mean absolute destruction, for as it is moving more and more out of balance, it cannot be easily compensated.

This event that you are about to experience is not to the degree that has been experienced many times upon the earth. Your earth has had this experience on many occasions. It is that your historical records did not survive, and so you do not understand it.

Your geological records have survived. *Your geologists are understanding that this is not something that is new. But it is outside of your conscious awareness, and it is outside of your current creativity. However, that which you experience in terms of participation upon the earth is not outside of your creative control. You may visualize yourself surviving in joy -- and that will be your experience.*

You have entered into many agreements as you came to planet earth. You have agreed to experience gravity. You have agreed to experience physicalness. You see, in your nonphysical dimension you merge in and out with one another. Here, you bang together. There are many things that you do from the nonphysical dimension that you do not do in the physical, and changing the shifting of the earth is just one of those, you see. And your Inner Being is complete with that.

Your Inner Being is knowing. Your Inner Being said, "I want to be a part of planet earth during this time of disruption, for I know that *new* brings opportunity for greater creativity. I know that when there is change, there is always stimulation of thought, and from stimulation of thought comes creation, and from creation comes joy. I am wanting to be a part of the experience of planet earth during this time of awakening, for I am wanting to experience the joy that will come forth as I find my blending, as well as the joy that will come forth as I experience it with others." You see?

You have lived many experiences upon this earth not so fulfilling as this one promises to be. For this is literally the time of AWAKENING. And the shifting of the earth is a part of it. It is a part of the reason that there will be more wanting to understand, you see. From your inner standpoint, you have created it, and you would not stop it, for you want the survival of this earth. You understand how long it takes an earth to become inhabitable. It is a very long process, you see. You are not wanting to give it up easily and start over again. And your conscious being agreed to all of that. It is just that it is hard to reconcile now. Perhaps our words will help. Are you clear?

QUESTION: If we can create within this thing, our physical, if we got the answer that our home is not safe -- can we intend for our home to be safe, could we create that?

ABRAHAM: That is similar to saying, "I am wanting that treasure. Not one like it, not one similar, but, that one." And at the same time another intends to have it, as well. And so, if the power of intent of this one is stronger than the power of that one, since there is only one prize, it is possible that this one could receive it. But, what you are wanting to create against, is that which has been set into motion at a greater level of creation, you see?

And you are much better off to intend to be in a safe place, than you are to intend that place to be safe.

QUESTION: OK. The other part of that, then, is that I know that my place and that my home is not safe. I mean, I've known this for a long time, so part of the creation that I've been working on, so intensely, and we've talked about it a lot, is another home. Now, I've come a long way, in that I realize that, and when I think of the shift, I can see me in no other place except this new place. I know all the details. I can see the furniture, I can see the walls, and everything.

Well, in the last two weeks though, since we spoke last, nothing is coming up. I mean, nothing. And I'm not even thinking about it intensely now.

I want to know what's happening? I still want it. I'm excited about it. I haven't changed my mind, I can see it vividly...

ABRAHAM: Have you experienced negative emotion regarding it?

COMMENT: No.

ABRAHAM: Then it will be. Release it and let it be. Trust the process. What more?

QUESTION: Where do animals come in?

ABRAHAM: It is a very broad subject. Your animals are wondrous, are they not? Your animals are beings, created in the way that you are, but with different agreements? They come forth as physical beings, as you do, and the energy that is coming through them is like your energy, but coming forth in a different way, with different intent.

To help you understand it, a little bit, we will tell you that there are animals who are actually experiencing energy that has been set forth from, perhaps, the same source as yours, although that is not a very common thing. In other words, it is possible for you to have an experience with a dog or a horse or a cat who is filled with the energy that has been set forth by, perhaps, your Inner Being who was wanting the experience of that, you see?

Your animals are responding from their Inner Beings, without conscious intervention, in a way that you are not able to do it. They are not consciously evolved as you are, and they respond in this physical environment more from inner knowing. It is what you call instinct.

COMMENT: You were talking about wishing or wish thinking, or whatever.

ABRAHAM: We are talking about creating.

COMMENT: Earlier, you were talking about, "If you wish it to be, it will be. Concentrating on, or believe it..."

ABRAHAM: Set forth your thought, and it will be.

QUESTION: OK, and you were talking about, in the spirit world, you know, they go through each other. By believing and concentrating on that, can you, in your physical body, go through something, like an out of body experience?

ABRAHAM: Indeed. But when you are in an out of body experience -- you are out of your body.

Are you knowing how much you wanted to be *in* that body? Out of body experiences are interesting to us, for we are knowing how much you wanted to be in that body, and so it interests us as you are trying to get out of it all the time! What more?

QUESTION: I just wondered. Is there really a spiritual hierarchy, and can you tell me about (Proper Name)?

ABRAHAM: *There is not a hierarchy in the way that you are thinking that there is. There is just constant evolvement. There is no ending to growth, you see? And there is not someone keeping score about how well you are doing. And there is no judgement or comparison.*

THERE IS JUST JOYOUS LIFE EXPERIENCE, YOU SEE.

And there are many beings that we are not aware of by name. We are not knowing this one. Are you?

COMMENT: I just heard that he was the "Planetary Logos" or that he was the being that had, in essence, come, and through his thought is...

ABRAHAM: He is the "greatest one of them all?"

COMMENT: Yes.

ABRAHAM: Indeed. There are many of those. What else? (Group laughter)

QUESTION: Abraham, the first part of February, I was in

Colorado on business, but had some time to spend alone, and during this time of reflection, it came to me that I wanted to go back to a simple life. That I was not happy the way my life was now. And when I came back, I came back with a happy intent of doing that. Is this event that's coming, going to put me in that simple life?

ABRAHAM: Indeed it is. Have any of you ever been in an environment where you went to school, and it was announced that the furnace was broken, and that there would be no school today?

COMMENT: Yay! (Group laughter)

ABRAHAM: And the reason you say "yay" is because there is not another who has planned this day for you. Your mother has released you to school. The school has released you to your mother, and you -- for this day -- are free. Free to be or do whatever you choose, and if you have had that experience, you remember the ecstasy that came upon you as you realized that you could, for the first time in a very long time, be the creator of your experience -- and that is what you are all about to experience.

You are about to experience a time when you will do that which is most important to you, instead of creating all of those experiences that please someone else, or that you have set forth at a time when your intentions were different, you see. It is your time to decide what it is that you are wanting in this day and to have it, you see.

It is a time when more beings, simultaneously, will be the deliberate creators of their experience, for there is very little of that occurring now.

Most of you are creating out of habit. Going through the motions of life, not receiving contentment, for contentment comes only from one place. Contentment comes only from intending and allowing and receiving. But as you are banging around, doing everything because somebody else thinks it is the thing to do, but not doing it because you want to do it -- you receive very little contentment from that.

This time that is before you is the time of greatest joy that you have ever experienced in this physical environment, or in any other, and you are right. It will be a time of simplicity, for the confusion will be severed.

All of the red tape, all of the communication, all of the technology that binds you to one another, will be temporarily severed, and you will be able to breathe and make decisions about how much of it you want to participate within again.

You are part of the rebuilding, you see. And we have a very famous statement. We are stating it enough, it is becoming famous, and that is: Sometimes it is of value to live in a house with not enough closets so that you are knowing that the next house that you are choosing will have more closets, you see. And so, as you have lived life experience, there are many parts of it that you are saying, "I am not wanting this."

ABRAHAM: What you are most wanting is freedom, and many of you are bound to the physical things that you have accumulated -- for they have taken your freedom away from you.

You do your greatest creating from wanting. And most of you spend most of your time suppressing your wanting. You see? You want only a little You don't want too much, for you are not wanting to experience the disappointment of wanting and not getting.

Because you don't understand what makes you get and what makes you not get, because you don't understand how you are getting what you are getting, you have withdrawn, and because you are not understanding that you are creator of your experience and controller of that which you will receive, you make no decisions, so that you do not become Selective Sifter, and then you receive some of everything.

And you are part of a world that has evolved to the state of overwhelment. Overwhelment because you are receiving all of this that means nothing to you, and you are stifling the decision of what is important to you, you see.

And this opportunity, in fact, this chosen opportunity, this very much wanted opportunity, this insisted upon opportunity...You are not here because you sort of wanted to be here. You are not here because you were the lucky one. You are here in physical form at this time because you said, "I want it," and you wanted it enough and allowed it enough that -- splat -- here you are. (Group laughter) And as you are here in this physical form, you are upon the brink of the most joyous of all experiences.

And you are right, it will be more simple. *Simplicity brings you your greatest joy. Complexity brings you your greatest distress.*

QUESTION: I would like some help bridging something. I have this thing...I had a very graphic dream last night that brought this forward, it's a belief that's blocking the creation that I'm working on, it's something that I live with every day in my life, and so, I'd like the tools to get past it. And what it is, is the belief that there's not enough.

OK, when I sit down to pay my bills, there's never enough money. When my son asks me for his prom, or senior ring, there's never extra money, or never enough money. This is something, you know, when I go to store my food, there's never enough money, there's no extra money, it's something I deal with on a daily basis. Now, I want to bridge that and get past it.

ABRAHAM: Good. We are wanting you to know how much appreciation we have for the clarity of your expression, for you are speaking in physical words, that which you are feeling -- and it is most remarkable.

Now, "There is never enough."

COMMENT: It's been my experience since birth.

ABRAHAM: Indeed. Hear the power of your words.

COMMENT: I know.

ABRAHAM: You have stated it perfectly. "There is never enough." And as you set forth those words, "There is never enough..."

That is enough, we will not say it again. (Group laughter)

Now, here is the bridge: "There has not been enough. That has been my experience. But that was before I understood what I understand now. Now, I know that there is enough, for I see it in others. I see others doing things with money that I would not do. (wasting it) I know that there is an abundance of money. And I know that I will find a way to begin attracting it into my experience. There is enough. It is just that I have not, to this point, attracted it, and I am in the process of doing that, now. I know that there is enough. I know that there is more than enough.

"I know that there is not one 'pot of gold' that everyone must dip into. But that we are the creators of abundance, and the the universe will supply all that is wanted by all of us who will allow it. And so, I see this never-ending waterfall of abundance, and while I have gone to the waterfall, most of my life, with a very little container, I am recognizing, now, that it has only been that I have taken a very small container. There is enough for all of us. I am not depriving another if I take a larger container. It is not that it is not there; it is that I have not taken a large enough container to allow more. And so, now I am. I am opening a wider passageway for the receiving of more abundance," you see.

"And while there has not been enough in the past, there will be more than enough in the future, for that is my current desire, and I am creator of my experience. There is more than enough. There is more than enough. THERE IS MORE THAN ENOUGH. There is more than enough. There is more than enough." And it will be yours. You are feeling the emotion.

COMMENT: Oh yes.

ABRAHAM: And we are as well.

ANOTHER COMMENTS: So am I. (Group laughter)

ABRAHAM: There is some for you too. And for you, and for you.

COMMENT: It was the container that was the problem. (Everyone talking at once, with much enthusiasm, about taking trucks and barrels to the waterfall...)

ABRAHAM: Do not take a truck or a barrel. Open your passageway. Open your passageway and allow it to flow in a never ending and continuous stream. All that you are wanting.

COMMENT: Thank you.

ABRAHAM: Indeed.

QUESTION: So what would be the best and most positive expression to have or to offer to someone when they come to me?

ABRAHAM: The greatest value that you can be to any other is to see them as perfect beings, as they are. And to encourage them to think and speak more of what they are wanting. And as they come to you expressing that which you know they do not want, say to them, *"I have come to know how powerful my words and thoughts are, and yours are very powerful, as well. And so, as you are speaking to me of that which you are not wanting, I must ask you to stop, for I am not wanting to assist you in your negative creating. Let us talk about what you want."*

And they will say to you more of what they don't want, for it is habit, you see, and you say, "No, you don't understand. I am very serious about this. *We must speak of what we are wanting, not of what we are not wanting."*

And soon they will recognize that when they speak of what is not wanted, that your ears will be closed.

Have you ever talked to anyone, and you could tell they were not listening? They are looking over your head, or down at their fingers, they are not paying attention to what you are saying, and when that happens to you, how do you feel? You no longer want to talk to them. Now, your friends, who are drawn to you, when they recognize you are not listening, will go somewhere else, you see? They will get the point from you.

You see, your words are powerful, but your example is even more powerful. Be who you are. Express what you know.

We have promised you a process that will assist you in the deliberate creating of your life experience on a day to day, or even moment by moment, basis. You see, when you understand that your thoughts create, then it is of great value for you to intentionally set forth your thought. Ideally, it would be good if you could do it in every moment, but that is a bit cumbersome, and so, what we encourage is that you divide your day into segments, into natural segments, and at the beginning of each of those segments, that you state clearly to yourself what it is that you are intending within it, you see.

Segments would be such as, when you get into your automobile, to go from one place to another. That is a segment. When you answer the telephone, it begins a new segment. If someone walks into the room, it begins a new segment. As you are brushing your teeth, it begins a new segment. Do you see what we are saying? And if you will take a moment at the beginning of that segment and say, "What I am wanting now, is clear communication as I am expressing to this being on the telephone." Then that which you are wanting to express will come forth properly. There are basically only two things that keep you from doing that which you intend, influence of others, or your own old habits, but as you have taken a moment to intend clearly what it is that you are wanting, then you will be less likely to be swept up by the influence of others, you see. And so that is the point of that. And so, anything that you are wanting within any segment of your day, if you will take a moment and state it clearly, then it will be. You see?

COMMENT: Yes, I understand. In other words, you're saying, instead of taking what's coming toward you, you think about what you want?

ABRAHAM: Indeed, Now, when you get into your automobile, as you are buckling your safety belt, see yourself arriving at your destination safely, refreshed, on time, you see.

As you are intending safety, be certain that which you are intending and thinking of is safety. Do not envision an accident and say, "I do not want that." For your thoughts attract that which you set forth.

And so, the key in all of this creating is to see it as you want it to be. We started to say, see the ending, but there is no ending. But see it as far as you can see it. See yourself arriving at whatever destination. See yourself with a balance in your checkbook that is more to your liking. Envision yourself going to your bank with much more than you are usually going with. See yourself balancing your checkbook and delighted with the very large balance that is there after everything else has been paid. Begin setting forth those pictures that are as you want them to be, and ask for the confirming positive emotion at the same time.

You see, when you understand the power that your emotion brings, then you will be faster at creating that which you want. When you sort of want something, it lumbers along on its way to you. And most often you have lost interest in it long before it arrives, and so it never arrives, or when it does it is no big deal. But those things that you want very much, those things that excite you very much, come into your life experience very quickly.

And so, as you are intentionally setting forth this vision of that which you are wanting to receive, bring yourself to an emotional state of excitement about it. Envision yourself, one after another, excluding those payments, see yourself writing "done." See yourself discarding. See it as complete, and feel the enthusiasm that comes forth as you do that. See yourself with much more accumulated. See yourself accumulating all of this, you see. Do whatever it takes to get yourself excited about it.

You have been focusing upon the lack. Therefore creating more of the lack. That is very common, particularly in regards to money. Let us tell you something about your financial situation as a people, not as individuals. For it is something that we are seeing a great deal of.

Contentment comes from allowing and then receiving...You want it; you allow it; you receive it; and the contentment that comes forth, comes only from that process.

You receive no contentment from something that someone else has created. It is only your wanting it and receiving it that brings forth contentment, you see. *Now, when you are intending the creation of something, and you create it by creating debt, then the creative process is out of balance, for now that which you have wanted you have received, but now you have the giving or the repayment or the creating, still to do, with the receiving already done,* do you see what we are saying?

COMMENT: How did you know? (Group laughter)

ABRAHAM: And so, there is not satisfaction. (It is because we have seen another. Quite a few others.) In this time in your nation, it has been a time of what you are all calling "easy credit." A time when the loans were offered very easily, you see, and so, without knowing, without even realizing, there was great debt that was accumulated.

And now there is not much satisfaction in repaying the debt, for the reward, or the receiving, has long come and gone. In many cases, you can't even remember what it was that you received for all of this, you see.

Now, here is the key to that. You have, in effect, lived in a house with not enough closets, and now you are knowing you are wanting closets, in other words, you are wanting the freedom from that debt, you see, and so, now you must create a new wanting. You must stimulate in yourself an excitement for being free of that debt. You must see yourself excitedly accumulating more dollars than are required, you see? And as you set this new wanting in place, there will be new satisfaction that comes forth as you are, one by one, taking care of those, you see. They have become oppressive because you have not allowed them to be something that is wanted. They have been something that you needed to do, and you must understand that wanting and needing are opposite.

When you are creating toward your wanting, there is enthusiasm and excitement. When you are creating toward your need, it is negative creating. And so, turn it, in your mind, into something that is very much wanted -- and what you are wanting is freedom, are you not? You are wanting the freedom from that. You are wanting to have the excess dollars, and so, as you will envision freedom, and get excited about that, and envision that which excites you about it as you are tearing it up and saying, "It is done," it will be, and much more quickly than you have imagined it thus far. Good.
What more?

COMMENT: Well, I want to say thank you for being able to come here, because what I get, every time that I come here and I ask a question, is that confirming -- because I've been writing about the freedom, and all of that, and every single time I get the confirmation, and I really appreciate that.

ABRAHAM: It is nice to know that we are as smart as you.

COMMENT: It is nice to have you. Thank you.

COMMENT: There was a statement you made just a moment ago, and it was something about fulfilling an intention you made at another time...It triggered something, back as part of the evolution of us as individuals, that we still maintain the ability and, indeed, the practice of changing our intentions from moment to moment, and that, perhaps, if we don't exercise that option and we let patterns from before prevail, we, some of us, can blame it on Karma.

ABRAHAM: Indeed, we call it Karma Kopout: "I'm fat in this life because I starved to death in the last. (Group laughter) Well, if I must blame myself, why not blame myself, but not *this* self. Let us blame one that no one can see."

QUESTION: If this disaster happens, there will be great amount of deaths, correct? A lot of people will die?

ABRAHAM: There will be some transition. About 50% of you...

QUESTION: Then we'll have an overload of spirits?

ABRAHAM: Don't worry about it. (Group laughter) From your inner perspective you see that as opportunity.

QUESTION: Abraham...manifestation here, and we have set, physical laws. Are those physical laws...can we change those physical laws?

ABRAHAM: Indeed. Not all at once.

QUESTION: As we accept that we can?

ABRAHAM: Indeed. You are part of the changing of a physical law. Perhaps, the first conscious awareness will be in this physical experience, and that is this:
     The creative energy that feeds your planet is being speeded up at a noticeable rate, and in this physical experience, you will be faster manifesters of thought, you see -- which is a good reason for you to start paying attention to the way that you feel so that you can focus your thoughts in the direction of that which is wanted.
     Did you notice that we did not say, so that you should start monitoring your thoughts. For that is very difficult, even impossible, but if you will pay attention to the way that you feel, then you will always create in the direction of that which is wanted. That is a physical law that has been accepted and has been experienced through very many generations of beings -- and in your lifetime you will see a change in that. And there are others.
     Perhaps, one day you will not have so much gravity. Perhaps, one day you will be able to blend your physical beings as you blend your Inner Beings, perhaps in your lifetime, if you are wanting it, and believing it.
     It is with great appreciation that we interact with you.

What we are wanting you to understand is something that you may not have thought of before: You see yourselves as beings who are here in physical form, wanting to receive knowing that is not part of your experience -- that is why you are ready to speak with your "dead" friends (Group laughter) -- and what we are wanting you to understand, is that not only do *you* benefit from the knowing that comes forth from us, but there is much benefit to ALL-THAT-IS as you are interacting here. For as this passageway is open, through which this interaction is occurring, and as you are individually opening your passageways, through which information and communication is occurring, your Inner Being and the Family that dwells therein and all that is connected to that -- which is literally all that there is -- for it is all one -- benefits by this experience, you see.

There is great love here for you. We are complete.

GROUP: Thank You!

ABRAHAM'S SPECIAL SUBJECT TAPES

Here are two sets of 10 ninety minute casettes, Volume I and Volume II. Each focuses, primarily, upon the listed topics, although Abraham does manage to "squeeze in" their basic overall message between the pointed questions presented by Jerry.

You can do no better, in order to build a foundation of understanding of Abraham's teachings, than to begin with tapes AB-1 through AB-4.

Singles, $9.95. Three or more at $7.75, or order five or more, in any one Volume category, and they will be shipped to you in a complimentary 10 space album.

AB-1 INTRODUCTION TO ABRAHAM

From this FREE, 90-minute introduction cassette, learn why Abraham has come to interact with physical man in this time. Hear an overview of Abraham's basic message and understand the important reasons for the recording of each of the cassettes listed here. Hear Jerry & Esther explain the process that led to their meeting of Abraham and how it has affected their personal life experience. Let this cassette guide you, selectively, to the perfect information that you seek.

ABRAHAM SPECIAL SUBJECT TAPES
VOLUME I

AB-2 LAW OF ATTRACTION -- The most powerful law in the universe. It affects every aspect of your daily life. A law which is, whether you understand that it is or not. Specific processes are offered here to help you learn how to harness this law -- to get what you want.

AB-3 LAW OF DELIBERATE CREATION -- Discover the ecstasy of understanding universal laws which are absolute -- no matter what the circumstances. Without an understanding of this universal law, it is as if you are playing in a game where the rules are not understood, so it is not only impossible to know if what you are doing is appropriate, but you do not know how to win the game. The rules of the game of life are clearly offered here.

AB-4 LAW OF ALLOWING -- Of all things that you will come to understand through this physical life experience, nothing is more important than to become an allower. In becoming an allower, you are free of the negativity that binds you. Learn the joyful difference between tolerating and allowing -- and experience the blissful difference in every relationship you have.

AB-5 SEGMENT INTENDING -- Our futures are individually paved by the steady stream of thoughts we set forth. We are literally creating our future life as we direct our thoughts of this moment into the future. Discover the magnificent power you hold in this moment -- and learn how to use that power always to your advantage.

AB-6 GREAT AWAKENING, BLENDING -- You have deliberately and excitedly chosen this time to be physical beings upon this planet, because you knew in advance that this would be the time when many -- not all -- physical beings would recognize the broadness and great value of their being. Follow this step-by-step process for awakening.

AB-7   RELATIONSHIPS, AGREEMENTS -- We are all creators as we individually think and plan, but we are also often co-creators as we interact with others. Most relationships with others are far less than we want them to be. Find out why. Discover how to rejuvenate unhealthy relationships and attract new harmonious ones.

AB-8   BODILY CONDITIONS -- Nothing is more important to us than the way we feel and look, and yet so many do not look or feel as they would like to. There is not a physical apparatus, no matter what the state of disrepair, that cannot have perfect health. Discover the powerful processes to bring your body to the state of being that pleases you.

AB-9   CHRIST CONSCIOUSNESS -- While it can be satisfying to read and remember the teachings of the great ones who have gone before us, it is ever more joyous to discover the power of that knowledge within our own being. Learn the process to go within -- as Christ encouraged -- to experience the blissful oneness with Christ.

AB-10   ADDICTIONS -- Habits, or compulsions, or addictions can range from annoying to destroying. Often, long after they are no longer wanted, they can bind and control your life. As you listen to this recording -- you will for the first time understand exactly what the addiction is, and the simple process offered here will free you from it.

AB-11   JOYOUS SURVIVAL -- While there are seemingly earth shattering events occurring in greater frequency upon your planet, you need not be affected by them. Discover how to create and control your experience in this seemingly unstable environment.

ABRAHAM SPECIAL SUBJECT TAPES VOLUME II

AB-12 PIVOTING & POSITIVE ASPECTS -- If I am the "Creator of my own experience", why don't I have more of what I want? Fostered by an action oriented world, most of you do not understand your true nature of attraction, thus the confusion in why you are getting what you are getting. These processes of pivoting and the book of positive aspects will assist you in the self-discovery of what is important to you, and will put you in the strong, clear place of well-being, so that you can allow what you want into your experience.

AB-13 SEXUALITY -- Love, sensuality and the perfect sexual experience -- pleasure vs. shame. This misunderstood issue lies at the heart of more disruption in the lives of physical beings than any other issue. Discover the true nature of your being, and release yourself from the negative turmoil that surrounds the subject of sexuality.

AB-14 DEATH -- Aging, deterioration and the perfect death experience — choices vs. chances. The gathering of years is a natural experience. However, deterioration of your physical body is neither natural nor necessary. Be healthy and productive and active and happy until the very day of your chosen re-emergence into the nonphysical.

AB-15 DOLLARS -- Abundance, in perfect flow -- gaining the freedom that dollars can bring vs. losing your freedom while gaining your dollars. As there is an abundance of the air you breathe, so there is an abundance of the dollars you seek. Listen and learn how to relax and breathe in the fresh air of freedom offered to you through the abundant flow of dollars.

AB-16 HEALTH, WEIGHT & MIND -- The perfect states of weight, health and mind -- how can I get there and stay there? Diet plans abound and research continues and yet the number of those unsuccessful at maintenance of satisfactory bodily and mental conditions increases steadily. Understand how your body functions and why you are as you are -- and then begin your swift and steady progress toward that which you desire.

AB-17 MATING -- The perfect mate: getting one, being one, evoking one -- Attracting vs. attacking. While it is your natural endeavor to co-create with others, there are few who have discovered the bliss of magnificent relationships. Find out how you can experience the joy of a perfect union.

AB-18 PARENTING -- Perfect harmony between my children and me -- and me and my parents. Harmonizing vs. traumatizing. While often disconnected from parents, either by death or by distance, your parent/child relationships often have great influence in your experience with your children or with your current life experience. Learn how to perceive what has been in a way that is beneficial to your now rather than destructive. Let that which you have lived be of value.

AB-19 CAREER -- The perfect career. What, where and when is it -- and what can I do about it now? With so many exterior standards or rules regarding the appropriateness of your behavior or choices -- in most cases more confusion than clarity abounds. Use this process to discover and at-tract that which is perfect for you. Stop the futile backwards approach -- and begin creating from the inside out.

AB-20 SELF APPRECIATION -- If I am so "Perfect as I am" -- then why don't I feel better about me than I do? Selfishness vs. selflessness. Your awareness of your perfection was intact as you emerged into this physical body, but it was soon sabotaged by the critical, comparing, judgmental world that surrounded you. Rediscover your true sense of value and well-being and perfection.

AB-21 INNER GUIDANCE -- Tell me more about my inner voice? Because you have thought in terms of being dead or alive, you forget that you are, simultaneously, physically focused while another part of you re-mains focused from nonphysical perspective. Once remembering that the inner you exists, you may begin to listen to what your Inner Voice is offer-ing. Here is the process for re-establishing that important conscious connection.

G-SERIES TAPES — PROGRESSIVE

Here is an opportunity for you to experience Abraham beyond the printed word. Almost like being there, you can mentally sit in on an Abraham dialogue and hear the tones of love and humor and strength that carry forth their consensual wisdom.

90 minute cassettes, composites of three-hour group sessions, these power packed messages will carry you forward, one giant step at a time, to your understanding and utilization of whatever aspects of Abraham's teachings that you are wanting to apply to your current experience.

These G-series tapes address many more topics than are listed here, but these listed points are -- in our opinion -- those that are addressed for the first time, or from a different perspective than we have previously heard.

Due to their progressive format, they are perfect for an ongoing study -- singly or in a group -- of Abraham's evolving teachings. We would suggest beginning with G-7-8-90 and then progressing forward.

Published quarterly in sets of ten, you may order one tape at $9.95, 3 or more at $7.75 -- or order 5 or more, in any one Season category, and receive a complimentary (while they are available) 10 space cassette album.

G-SERIES TAPES, SUMMER, 1990

G-7-8-90 Comprehensive session to a Unity Group. Where does mental depression originate? How can I reverse a negative momentum? A practical process: "To be, To have, To do." Homeless, free & misdirected guilt. But, what about the little ones? Seatbelts, meat & mental ghostbusters.

G-7-15-90 An update on the use of universal power. From vitamins to exercise to death. Why? How does a person attract prejudice? Dollars, freedom & your balance of thought. So, is it precognition or precreation? Overwhelmed? A 15 minute solution. What to do when you don't know what to do.

G-8-1-90 Family crises, in-laws, outlaws & babies. How trying too hard works against you. How to have the gain without the pain. Comparison as your death trap. Why a common cold doesn't take your life. What is our duty to enlighten others? Why does sex seem to cause such trouble?

G-8-3-90 How to "resist" resisting and allow allowing. The unique attraction of Abraham. An experience with a frivolous entity. Health -- Deformities -- Plagues & AIDS. The meaning of love. What is our work? A powerful closing affirmation.

G-8-19-90 The power of the Book of Positive Aspects. When action makes it worse. Health and the effects of genetics. Iraq and the USA -- a perspective. Use the "Wallet Process" to attract $. Why don't all fears manifest? A fun, feel-good closing.

G-8-22-90 Competition as a motivator? The building of your body. What is the significance of pain? Illness created to justify death. Action as a justification for being. Take dollars out of the struggle. A beautiful closing affirmation.

G-9-7-90 Why do Indians pray to not be reborn? Who created the GOD who created the GOD? Preschool, prebirth and creating worlds. Be in your prime on the day you die. How to avoid a predicted outcome. An opinion on a 12 Step Program. Forming an Abraham study group?

G-9-9-90 Why is reacting a hindrance? How does the universe hear us? What happened when I quit trying. Example of the power of thought over action. Healing, medicine, diet & the arthritis gene. Crystals, Leprechauns & little bones. Reincarnation from a point of misery.

G-9-19-90 Don't look for the cause. Results of negative motivation. How can I elude the economic cycle? Cool water on hot, tired feet. Blocks of thoughts vs. words. Is gambling a gamble? Doing for another ...is saying....

G-9-23-90 What makes Abraham feel good? What does Abraham want? Health, heredity & blocks of thought. When language deceives. Stay off the scales. Wheat circles mystery. Have fun. Trust the process.

G-SERIES TAPES, FALL, 1990

G-10-3-90   Process to bridge or modify conflicting beliefs.   A grasshopper & the power of attraction. Some positive aspects of a fear of cancer. Sympathizing & Empathizing vs. Helping. Tired? A process for regaining energy. Do we attract nice people -- or nice from people? Prophets, predictors & prognosticators.

G-10-5-90   Dreams, blocks of thought & your reality.   Jealousy, polygamy & warning bells. The value of making more decisions. Is there truly an accidental death? Homosexuality, and why it is chosen. How to create your unlimited new vision. Invisible counselors & the 4 minute mile.

G-10-7-90 Weight control, flu & fever blisters. The Prime Minister & the fairies of the universe. The ecstasy of your Inner Being in your now. Which comes first, the thought or the feelings? The process of personal upliftment. Why most diets don't work. Your metabolism responds to your thought.

G-10-20-90 Mutuality of Moses, Jesus, Muhammad & Mormonism. Working hard to succeed defies the Universal Laws. Happiness. You can't give it if you don't have it. What is the real source of good & evil? Esther, her Spiritual Guide and the physical focus. A brief history of the formation of religion. How man's insecurity creates man's bondage.

G-10-27-90 Use the opposition to benefit your cause. Are animals here with a purpose? You can run, but you still take you with you. Linear lives vs. The Eternal Now. An interpretation of that which you call GOD. How to create a positive divorce experience. Life is supposed to be fun!

G-11-2-90 Power in a night's sleep and a new beginning. Power in understanding and utilizing the Laws. Power in your choices, emotions and expectations. Power in inspired action & personal energy. Powerful formula for a pure new beginning. What gives the Tar Baby its power to hold you? Powerful feel-good affirmations.

G-11-24-90 Foods, health, beliefs & bulls in a china shop. How can I receive dollars without working for them? A test & 100 yard dash through 100 closed doors. Carrot devas, Abraham, Peter Pan and other labels. Genetic & atomic engineers -- & our choices. Evolution & the four billionth monkey. Why do some native tribes remain primitive?

G-12-7-90 Why the variety in cataclysmic expectations? Battering rams & other door openers. How much wanting is too much to want? The Harmonic Chameleon. Jesus, Christmas & the horror of a poor basket. What is the purpose of a physical brain? Abraham's version of "The Christmas Story."

G-12-14-90 Allergies & hands-on healing. Rapists, light shows & birds of a feather. Why are there so many rabbits? A process to begin new thought habits. Intent vs. cellular mob rule. The deer-slayer: one's meat, another's poison. Pre-emergent intents & my highest priority.

G-12-29-90 How to want and not feel the deadly lack. So, who has the final answers? The way to positively leave a negative group. Memory? Your mind is not for storage. Love, and how it can be evoked. Take one of these the first thing in the morning. Abundance, via taking money out of the equation. Castles, shacks, money and other delightful stuff.

G-SERIES TAPES, WINTER 90-91

G-1-4-91 Use this guided process for daily use. It doesn't have to be hard to be important. Your guarding sabotages your experience. Do you measure your worth by your stuff? How can you get more money than you expect? A perfect being in a state of becoming. Good can't come when having a hard life.

G-1-5-91 Can't give a charge from a dead battery. Valuable words for a hospital visit. Sympathy cards and the Law of Attraction. The planting of the arthritis seed. Earning your food vs. manna from heaven. Freedom and empowerment vs. control. Loyalty vs. living in the moment.

G-1-13-91 Does Abraham have a beginning source? The creation and evolution of the planet. How a willingness to die attracts death. Wars, games and unarmed noncombatants. Is there any value in painful therapy? Aging, expectancy and nursing homes. Courage is usually spoken of by cowards.

G-1-26-91 How can I change my self-image? What is the value of an aptitude test? Practical advice to live one full day. A cremation, a bird, and tears of joy. A perception of that which is called GOD. Finding peace in a search for paradise. How much can be gained from one tape?

G-2-8-91 Any of our insecurity from past lives? If nonphysical is so great, why return? Birth, and the crack of least resistance. Seeing each day as a mini-lifetime. A cosmic continuation of consciousness. How are we drawn to prehistoric sites? The value of a near death experience.

G-2-16-91 Can I empower my creation with emotion? I want all joy; what attracts confusion? What is the significance of sleep? Procrastination, as a positive non-action. Is pain of value to our growth? A dad's death and a white dove. A scenario for a sculpted body.

G-2-17-91 How can I uplift, as Abraham uplifts? Using a piece of twine to dock a ship. Inner guidance and your ultimate goal. Should there be greater purpose than joy? How to sift through the inner chatter. The correlation between money and freedom. When is the worst time to take action?

G-2-23-91 Do you want to "make" someone happy? When is it too late to begin? Why does the negative have "power"? How to experience a good nights' sleep. How much negative is too much? Warnings as self-fulfilling prophecies.

G-3-1-91 Joy as resonant with Inner Being. What is all this talk about beliefs? Is there any unrealistic desire? Fear and confusion and the inner voice. Society and its influence toward disease. The appropriateness of medicine. Abraham, and the Ten Commandments.

G-3-8-91 How much of me to "sacrifice" to my family? How appropriate is self-discipline? Why is there a seeming enthusiasm for war? Esther, and the symphony of Abraham. Am I this me through all of time? Prospective: Big ones eat little ones. The relativity of staying happy.

G-SERIES TAPES, SPRING, 1991

G-3-10-91 Why no one can take your freedom away. How both allowing and resisting create. Can we communicate with one in a coma? How can we best step back into positive? Do you feel best doing what doesn't earn $? Particular about your thoughts as your actions? How to know what makes you happy.

G-3-23-91 Your being here justifies your being here. Having and doing as an enhancement of being. Who created Universe? Attraction of abundance, continued. The joy and power of aligned priorities. In the flow, vs. a foot in two philosophies.

G-4-6-91 Leave "spiritual" to the angels. Is spirituality compatible with wealth? Objectivity as your downfall. Pain as a cultural perception. Should we ignore history? How to tune out lower priorities. Aging as evolving, versus deteriorating.

G-4-19-91 Wanting to change others, binds you. An aura of a positive pacifist. The value of a classroom leader. Children are not mere children. A definition of "JOY". How to keep fear from sneaking in. Nothing is important enough to feel bad.

G-5-4-91 Stage fright and fear of evaluation — a solution. Some facets of LOVE — continued. Co-dependencey and feeding not-enoughness. Parent/child punishment relationship. Spare the rod and spoil the classroom? American morality in the 90's. The value of rebellious teens.

G-5-5-91 Counterparts, Counterselves & Counterpoints. A child's perspective of Universe. What can the devil make us do? The detrimental aspects of statistics. Why hiding doesn't work. How can we do without doing? Which actions produce stress?

G-5-24-91 Feel good — nothing is more important. Why you have nothing to defend against. Do you heal faster asleep or awake? The cost of a free health exam. Universe wasn't created through action. How much is too much from Inner Being? Birds, beasts and joy begetting joy.

G-6-1-91 Is having a back-up plan a sabotage? You didn't come to stay forever. A teacher, tuning forks & harmonic expectations. Is an imaginary playmate imagined? The leading edge of creation. Could Abraham conduct a symphony? Wellness and the crack of least resistance.

G-6-2-91 How did Jerry & Esther get this happy? Testing, as a form of disbelief. Is TALENT an unexplainable gift? Is it OK to kill for fun? Handicapped, and the value of beingness. How to overcome unwanted habits. Selfish love, it feels so good.

G-6-7-91 The advantage of self-adoration. Appropriateness of a reverence for life. How and why we attract birth conditions. Are there malfunctioning nonphysicals? Freedom, GROWTH & joy or freedom, growth & JOY? On-the-job self-empowerment. Joyful becoming vs. seeking endings.

G-SERIES TAPES, SUMMER, 1991

G-7-4-91 A morning process to vibrate self to ecstasy. A new game: "A Day of Yeses." When your "go power" has got up and gone. Jerry, a scorpion, and Inner Guidance. The fittest survive vs. meek inherit the earth. The value of birth as a new beginning. A Chiropractor, and reducing sublimated thoughts.

G-7-20-91A Feel good in a negative family situation. Destructive overeating as an action from lack. Guilt: the separation of you and Spirit. The cause of most business failures. How to vibrate in harmony with what you want. To see every day as a positive new beginning. That ominous, anonymous, unidentified fear.

G-7-20-91B Cause of a general feeling of well-being. An instant manipulation of your reality? The eternal abundance of Universe. Being selfish enough to feel good. Synchronicity, Esther, and a crashing boulder. Deadlines, and eating green tomatoes. To change the balance of thought regarding $.

G-8-10-91 With a Unity Church group in Colorado. To control an uncontrollable anger. Career, and how to trust without testing. Have we any obligation to be happy? Can you get poor enough to enrich the poor? "Thou shalt not kill," under what conditions? When to seek medical attention?

G-8-11-91 A word from one "back from the dead." How resisting the unwanted, disallows the wanted. Commitment, as a form of entrapment. How to get out of bed on the right vibration. Why most can't just die in their sleep. How to have the best sex of a lifetime. Planning a disruptive family encounter?

G-8-23-91 Are some persons energized by negatives? Primary intents & the only joyous way to fly. Can foods, herbs, etc., raise your vibrations? Feelings, as a barometer of your vibrations. Is it random, or is it synchronistic? A process to open a positive avenue to $. A superb, uplifting, comprehensive closing.

G-8-25-91 How can I fan the flame of my passion? What can I do to cause it to happen fast? Abortion, an issue of right or wrong? Depression, and the drugs that treat it. Do thoughts without feelings create? The universal cats don't hear "no." Whose opinion do you value, yours or theirs?

G-8-26-91 Automatic writing, an appropriate experience? Do you feel an abundance blockage? Why wars to end all wars don't. To positively cocreate when mate's wants differ. How to sell the "unsalable." A Psychotherapist's pain in working with pain. Happy haunters and metaphysical panthers.

G-8-31-91 Abraham's favorite subject: Deliberate Creating. Creation, as 99% complete before seeing any evidence. Value in acquiring patience? Fishing a bucket of Casper from an ocean of beingness. Objectivity, as a damper to higher vibrations. Why so many centuries before these teachings? Can we be all one and yet maintain individuality?

G-9-1-91 The quandary of a yearly health checkup. A metaphysical perspective of tooth cavities. Find what holds one back? Focus on unwanted and perpetuate unwanted. Is looking back a waste of life? To resolve the pain of Vietnam participants. Regurgitation vs. your Supreme Guidance System.

G-SERIES TAPES, FALL, 1991

G-9-14-91 The synchronicity of Divine Inspiration. The non-semantics of nonphysicality. Are you always open to vibratory influence? Why protection doesn't feel good. Depression as an absence of Inner Being. The significance of a smiling mother hen. True motivation is empowering.

G-9-20-91 The attraction of a suitable partner. Why you can't suffer your way to joy. Justified negativism as a miscreator. The positive message in a negative emotion. A Process for wellness. When your chicken part drives your car. A teacher is bothered by would-be truants.

G-9-21-91 Sleep as a re-emergence into the nonphysical. How addressing the problem perpetuates the problem. Food and sex, as practical and sensual. The justice of a massacre to "avert" a massacre. How to identify great deeds. Physical matter as an extension of refined thought. Abraham addresses the "frivolousness of feeling good."

G-9-22-91 Placebos, Perceptions and Formulas for Miracles. To vibrationally double your dollars. Basic Abraham in 800 words or less. Why the diagnosis accelerates the diagnosed. A "scientific" perception of Esther's condition. Your guide to an appropriate diet. The power of your vibrations over world events.

G-9-28-91 Arthritis, how far does it run in a family? Independent prosperity in a mass negative economy. High energy children in this time of transition. The effect of television on our society. A dialogue on "high tech" health care. What are Abraham's "qualifications?" Resist not; relax into your well-being.

G-10-26-91 The key to breaking old unwanted habits. Nutrition, diet and spiritual and physical well-being. Are you ever aware of "presences" around you? How spiritual has the world become? Abraham's empowerment of a school child. Some modern day fairy tales. Esther's value as an example of thought reception.

G-10-27-91 The healing "tool" is not the issue. To enhance the ecstasy of sexual passion. "Financial independence" from what? How much joy can the body handle? Abraham counsels a counsellor regarding "therapy." An enlightening dialogue with a mother-to-be. Say "yes" to your tax dollars.

G-11-9-91 Which racial group has the most wisdom? Would you "drive it on the sidewalk?" So, who has the clearest guru? "Honey, you can't love five...and stay alive." What color of ink are you spewing? The choice between homo and hetero sexuality. Birth, and the justice of the universe.

G-11-10-91 When we expectantly ask to feel good. The quest for "The Historical Jesus," cont'd. The quest for "The Valid Virgin Mary," cont'd. Do drugs affect communication with Inner Being? The creative dynamics of a cluster of beings. An affirmation to affect others. Personal control vs. group standards regarding body shape.

G-11-30-91 To clarify reception from your Inner Being. Would you have the "handicapped" ones improve? Body cells, as responsive to mass consciousness. When should bickering family members cease communication? Words for someone disconnected from Inner Being. The attraction power of a state of appreciation.

G-SERIES TAPES, WINTER, 1991

G-12-7-91 Prayer, the power of, and a method of. Why do the rich get richer? Thought energy, and the perspectives of masses. Out of body experience, astral travels, etc. Can we feel good when conflicting ideas are thrust at us? Which is best, to give or to receive? Can we all allow all to be, have and do...?

G-12-8-91 The creative process and bridging of beliefs. Energy connection between man and beast. The counterproductivity of negative probing. Changing the future effects of past thought. A teenage child in the land of the free. Why there is no injustice on your planet. A dynamic dialogue on the Perception of Time.

G-1-18-92 If anything can go wrong, will it? See yourself as an energy funnel. Should we try to enjoy the unenjoyable? Are you mentally replaying unwanted scenarios? Your ability to perceive is always in the now. Seeing, or not seeing, neither validates nor invalidates. The universal wordless language.

G-1-25-92A Is my soul ever lost or alone? What is the best use of my time? Can I get poor enough to enrich the poor? Pain, as the extended allowance of negative emotion. Abraham's words to a new born baby. Should I form an "Abraham Fun Group"? Can you tell me how to be happy?

G-1-25-92B "Disturbed" children have much to teach you. Joyous mating vs. building monuments to pain. Words for one in fear of impending death. Free-will as an allowance of changing destiny. A process for the selection of a "life-partner." Marriage vows, by Abraham. Children, and the positive aspects of a divorce.

G-2-1-92 The paralysis of analysis. The empowerment of dollar-basking. Are you spending your psychic nest egg? Is not the jailer also jailed? Your greatest value to others is. Consider a world without law enforcement. Why isn't positive thought more dominant?

G-2-2-92 Are you wanting more peace and health? Consider advantages of a structured government. Why Abraham teaches meditation. Does a loved one attract distracting chaos. A wedding and the dilemma of protocol. Nonphysical memory of your physical vibration. Naught is more important than appreciation of self.

G-2-15-92 What if 100 monkeys believed in joy as the purpose? Turnabout of a parental happiness damper. A recipe for an Abraham stew. How can all find way back to their source? Words for a mediation group. You don't have to think of $ to have $.

G-2-16-92 Art and music in the nonphysical plane? What is the current state of the planet? If you feel emotional—it is important to you. How can we halt negative thought drift? To please the crowds, here is your message. You can't measure the quality of life by its length. To have a love affair with self.

G-3-21-92 When your lover doesn't want a serious relationship. If it makes you feel good to work hard—do it. Who are you when you are all alone? Are there still potent moments of self-doubt? Party Cat makes his timely entrance. What is your best decision to make right now? Rape, massacre—and other forms of disconnectedness.

G-SERIES TAPES, SPRING, 1992

G-4-11-92A What you can dig up but can't throw away. Caged by conformity to what-has-been. Deal with an arousal of an unwanted belief. How sleep saves you from self-destruction. A beautiful welcome to a new infant. The international economy as an illusion. Why is Abraham interacting with us?

G-4-11-92B Petroleum, and the justice of planetary balance. A body without need for sleep, food, air or water? Do Abraham's thoughts ever focus on lack? Ego. Fear. Guilt. Release or dissolve them? Beauty, deformity, and other perspectives. Perspective of Inner Being's experience through you. Something for you to believe in.

G-5-2-92A Rodney King, police beatings, video, verdict and riots. Los Angeles police, and brutality, as a perspective. A connected beings' effect as judge or jury. Where did civilization leave its natural path? Dreams, as blocks of thought from Inner Being. A process to empower the little ones. Did Los Angeles children attract the riots?

G-5-2-92B The Dead Sea Scrolls. They're back! Always in the right place at the right time? Beautiful words, for one who is "terminally ill." Wealth, spirituality...you can have it all. Heroism? Pain is not needed for growth. Why doesn't prosperity, health & joyousness come to all? To know in which direction to grow.

G-5-3-92 The empowering value of decision making. A short-cut process to feel your value. Allowing a loved one's withdrawal from physical. Preoccupied with issues of "right and wrong"? An unborn child's choice to not be physical? To help a negative child to pivot. Take all action from your place of feeling good.

G-5-9-92A The difference between tolerating and allowing. Why do we forget our pre-emergence agreements? More revealing perspectives of Rodney King & police brutality. Each thought sets a reality into motion. Why the time between thought and its manifestation? How can I achieve true "goodness"? See the "error of our ways" in nonphysical?

G-5-9-92B Health, as per Inner Being's alignment of cells. Value in seeking the cause of illness? Was there health before medical insurance? Different valid realities, physical and nonphysical? Reflect not past perception into your future. A message from your Inner Being. Do the disconnected ones create also?

G-5/22/92 It's nice to have a friend upstream. $ from playing, vs. working to earn $. Old beliefs wither as per new choices. A potential for ecstasy with many Soulmates. The cheap little car that couldn't. Enjoy the "why?", and let the "what" evolve. A perspective of nursing home tenants.

G-6-6-92A Choosing from physical while harmonizing with nonphysical. You get what you think about, wanted or not. Marching to the beat of a dysfunctional drummer. Sameness wasn't your vision, newness was. Conscience, established from a place of lack. Make more decisions in every day. When it's perfect, you'll feel exhilaration.

G-6-6-92B "Walk-ins, Piggy-backs, etc.", have no power to "attach." Talk to child about wanted, get "no" out of vocabulary. Teachers, as catalysts to student's connectedness. Parents, as entry into physical, not as guards. What inspires death defying sexuality? The beasts, as your best teachers. The purpose of your physical experience.

BOOKS BY ABRAHAM

BOOK -- A NEW BEGINNING I

This extraordinary book is powerfully offered into this physical dimension by a group of nonphysical teachers who call themselves Abraham. They express clearly and simply the laws of the universe, explaining in detail how we can deliberately flow with these laws for the joyful creation of whatever we desire. Abraham describes this as the time of awakening, explaining that each of us chose, with very deliberate intent, this specific time of great change to participate in this physical experience. An empowering, life-changing book that will assist you in seeing your personal life experience as you have never seen it before. -- $9.95

BOOK -- A NEW BEGINNING II

An uplifting book that strikes a cord with the very core of your being. Written by Abraham to assist you in understanding the absolute connection between your physical self and your inner self. Abraham puts this physical life experience into perspective as they explain and define who we really are, and why we have come forth as physical beings. This book is filled with processes and examples to assist you in making a deliberate conscious connection with your own Inner Being, that you might find the awesome satisfaction with this physical life experience that can only come once this connection is made. -- $9.95

Psychic space
Safe Zone ~ 198
intent - my family of non physical beings

HOW TO ORDER

Our order forms are for your convenience, and we will send a replacement order form back to you with each shipment. In order to assist in our efficient processing of your order, please:

- Print all information clearly, or type.
- List each item, its stock number (ie: AB-1) and its price.
- Pay with your personal check, money order, or use your MasterCard or Visa.

INTERNATIONAL ORDERS

Orders outside of the continental U.S. will be shipped US Postal Service (unless UPS is specified) and the additional shipping cost will be charged. Send U.S. funds only.

WE SHIP UPS OR US POSTAL

On larger orders of multiple tapes or books, UPS is usually the fastest, safest, most economical way, but we ship most smaller orders by U.S. Postal. Your order is normally packaged and shipped within 2 working days after we receive it.

PRICE CHANGES

Our posted prices may vary without notice as those who supply us with services or materials may change their prices to us without notice.

TELEPHONE CONSULTATIONS

To arrange a private telephone consultation with Abraham — in order to discuss some of their broader, clearer perspectives of your experience — call (512) 755-2299 and establish a time to call back and visit with Abraham. Your interactions or cocreations with others or with All-That-Is, your financial or business or work conditions, your physical well-being — or your over-all state of being...whatever you would like to discuss, your confidential call will be recorded, and the recording and invoice will be sent to you.

DEFECTIVE OR DAMAGED TAPES OR BOOKS

Should you ever receive, from us, a book that is damaged or a tape that is garbled, blank, bound or broken, please call or write and tell us the title or the series date and we will replace the item — or refund your cost. Due to the spontaneous group interaction with Abraham, the G-Series or W.T.P. or M.T.P. tapes can sometimes be varied in volume, so we just take the best — and ignore the rest. (We do intend to improve it, as we move forward)

PRICE LIST • ORDER FORM

ADD THESE SHIPPING COSTS	
The following shipping and handling rates apply within the continental U.S. Please add them to your item cost.	
Cost of item under 10.00	add 2.75
Between 10.00 and 30.00	add 3.90
Between 30.00 and 50.00	add 5.40
Orders over 50.00	add 6.70

We are most appreciative of the many suppliers of services and materials who make it possible for Abrahams' words to reach you so efficiently. As costs of doing business are increased, or decreased (taxes, inflation, etc.) to any of our suppliers and passed on to us, we, in turn, through our varied business transactions, reflect those changes back into the international economy.

PRICE LIST

- **CASSETTE TAPES** — $9.95 each. Order 3 or more at $7.75 each — or order 5 or more (in same "Volume" or "Season") and they will be shipped to you in a complimentary *, convenient 10 space cassette album. Abraham's Special Subjects 90 minutes, "AB Series" and their "G-Series" 90 minute group session composites are all priced the same: $77.50 for the album sets of 10, $9.95 singles or $7.75 each when ordering 3 or more. (Plus shipping & handling)

- **BOOKS** — $9.95 each. Take a 20% discount when ordering 3 or more. (Plus shipping and handing) Study groups, teachers or dealers, call for discount when ordering 9, or more, books.

- **TELEPHONE CONSULTATION WITH ABRAHAM** — Fee: $15 for the first 15 minutes (the minimum) and $2 per minute as you wish to continue past 15 minutes. (To discuss any vital personal issue — call [512] 755-2299 and set an appointment to call back. A recording of your confidential session will be mailed to you.)

- **MONTHLY TAPE PROGRAM (M.T.P.)** — $48 for 4 month subscription. One 90 minute composite, each month, that presents the most new practical material from Abraham, is selected and mailed to a group of subscribers (9.25 + 2.75 S/H)

- **WEEKLY TAPE PROGRAM (W.T.P.)** — $41 for 1 month subscription. Composites of 180 minute group sessions. 4 tapes. May be received over 4 to 6 weeks (7.50 + 2.75 S/H)

- **WORKSHOPS, WEEKENDS, SEMINARS** — Fees vary with times, lengths & locations. Posted in our newsletter, when booked far enough in advance, or call for activities in your area.

* a limited offer. 9/91

ORDER FORM

FILL OUT AND CALL IT IN TO: **(512) 755-2299**
After Nov., 1992 Area Code changes to **(210)**
OR MAIL TO: **ABRAHAM SPEAKS**
P.O. BOX 1706, BOERNE, TX 78006

NAME (Please print)_____

ADDRESS_____

CITY_____STATE_____

ZIP_____TEL_____

(To ship by UPS, we need your street or R.R. number—not a P.O box)

QUANTITY	STOCK NUMBER	ITEM	PRICE
	AB-1	TAPE: FREE INTRO TO ABRAHAM (S/H ONLY)	2.75
	ANBI	BOOK: "A NEW BEGINNING I" (@ 9.95)	
	ANBII	BOOK: "A NEW BEGINNING II" (@ 9.95)	
	VOL I	TAPE ALBUM: 10 SPECIAL SUBJECTS (77.50)	
	VOL II	TAPE ALBUM: 10 SPECIAL SUBJECTS (77.50)	
	G-SUMMER '90	TAPE ALBUM: 10 GROUP SERIES (77.50)	
SPECIAL SUBJECTS: AB-			
GROUP SERIES: G-			
	(If you need more space, add another sheet of paper)		

(S/H) SHIPPING & HANDLING RATES Continental U.S.A.		
Up to $10.00 . . . . . . add $2.75	**ADD TOTAL OF ITEMS**	
10.00 to 30.00 . . . . . .add 3.90	**ADD SHIPPING & HANDLING**	
30.00 to 50.00 . . . . . .add 5.40	(Subtract any quantity discounts)	
Over 50.00 . . . . add 6.70	(TX delivery, add 6.25% Sales Tax)	
	(Add/subtract credits or chgs)	
	TOTAL AMOUNT ENCLOSED	

[ ] PERSONAL CHECK (Make checks payable to: J & E Hicks)
[ ] MASTERCARD   [ ] VISA   [ ] OTHER

CARD #_____EXP DATE_____

NAME ON CARD (PRINT)_____

CARDHOLDER'S SIGNATURE_____

THANK YOU!

Our thanks to you for your role in this joyous cocreation. Your thoughts as we interact, your pondering, questioning, recognizing, knowing, wanting...your thoughts add to our forward motion and to the fulfillment of our purpose.

We intend to allow Abrahams' words of perspective, positive guidance, and stimulation of thought, to go as far and as fast as they are wanted, and at the same time, we intend to continue our abundant positive mental and material and spiritual experience — and we do appreciate your contribution of "thoughts, words and deeds."

Do you have a friend who would enjoy our newsletter?

Name (Please print)_____

Address_____

City/State/Zip_____

Do you participate with a progressive group? Would you like to engage Abraham & Esther & Jerry for a weekend or a workshop for your group? If so, we would like to hear from you. Comments:

YOUR UNCONDITIONAL
GUARANTEE OF SATISFACTION

We are aware that due to technical or personal idiosyncrasys you may receive a damaged or defective item from us — but we will replace it or refund your money (whichever you prefer) just as soon as you call or write and give us the details. Please don't bother with shipping the item back to us. Just toss it away. We want you to be completely satisfied with our products and our service.

Jerry & Esther

ORDER FORM

FILL OUT AND CALL IT IN TO: **(512) 755-2299**
After Nov., 1992 Area Code changes to **(210)**
OR MAIL TO: **ABRAHAM SPEAKS**
P.O. BOX 1706, BOERNE, TX 78006

NAME (Please print)_____

ADDRESS_____

CITY_____STATE_____

ZIP_____TEL_____

(To ship by UPS, we need your street or R.R. number—not a P.O box)

QUANTITY	STOCK NUMBER	ITEM	PRICE
	AB-1	TAPE: FREE INTRO TO ABRAHAM (S/H ONLY)	2.75
	ANBI	BOOK: "A NEW BEGINNING I" (@ 9.95)	
	ANBII	BOOK: "A NEW BEGINNING II" (@ 9.95)	
	VOL I	TAPE ALBUM: 10 SPECIAL SUBJECTS (77.50)	
	VOL II	TAPE ALBUM: 10 SPECIAL SUBJECTS (77.50)	
	G-SUMMER '90	TAPE ALBUM: 10 GROUP SERIES (77.50)	
SPECIAL SUBJECTS: AB-			
GROUP SERIES: G-			
(If you need more space, add another sheet of paper)			

(S/H) SHIPPING & HANDLING RATES Continental U.S.A.	
Up to $10.00 . . . . . . add $2.75	
10.00 to 30.00 . . . . . .add 3.90	
30.00 to 50.00 . . . . . .add 5.40	
Over 50.00 . . . . add 6.70	

ADD TOTAL OF ITEMS _____
ADD SHIPPING & HANDLING _____
(Subtract any quantity discounts) _____
(TX delivery, add 6.25% Sales Tax) _____
(Add/subtract credits or chgs) _____
TOTAL AMOUNT ENCLOSED _____

[ ] PERSONAL CHECK (Make checks payable to: J & E Hicks)
[ ] MASTERCARD   [ ] VISA   [ ] OTHER

CARD #_____EXP DATE_____

NAME ON CARD (PRINT)_____

CARDHOLDER'S SIGNATURE_____

THANK YOU!

Our thanks to you for your role in this joyous cocreation. Your thoughts as we interact, your pondering, questioning, recognizing, knowing, wanting...your thoughts add to our forward motion and to the fulfillment of our purpose.

We intend to allow Abrahams' words of perspective, positive guidance, and stimulation of thought, to go as far and as fast as they are wanted, and at the same time, we intend to continue our abundant positive mental and material and spiritual experience — and we do appreciate your contribution of "thoughts, words and deeds."

Do you have a friend who would enjoy our newsletter?

Name (Please print)_____

Address_____

City/State/Zip_____

Do you participate with a progressive group? Would you like to engage Abraham & Esther & Jerry for a weekend or a workshop for your group? If so, we would like to hear from you. Comments:

YOUR UNCONDITIONAL
GUARANTEE OF SATISFACTION

We are aware that due to technical or personal idiosyncrasys you may receive a damaged or defective item from us — but we will replace it or refund your money (whichever you prefer) just as soon as you call or write and give us the details. Please don't bother with shipping the item back to us. Just toss it away. We want you to be completely satisfied with our products and our service.

Jerry & Esther

ORDER FORM

FILL OUT AND CALL IT IN TO: **(512) 755-2299**
After Nov., 1992 Area Code changes to **(210)**
OR MAIL TO: **ABRAHAM SPEAKS**
P.O. BOX 1706, BOERNE, TX 78006

NAME (Please print)_____

ADDRESS_____

CITY_____STATE_____

ZIP_____TEL_____

(To ship by UPS, we need your street or R.R. number—not a P.O box)

QUANTITY	STOCK NUMBER	ITEM	PRICE
	AB-1	TAPE: FREE INTRO TO ABRAHAM (S/H ONLY)	2.75
	ANBI	BOOK: "A NEW BEGINNING I" (@ 9.95)	
	ANBII	BOOK: "A NEW BEGINNING II" (@ 9.95)	
	VOL I	TAPE ALBUM: 10 SPECIAL SUBJECTS (77.50)	
	VOL II	TAPE ALBUM: 10 SPECIAL SUBJECTS (77.50)	
	G-SUMMER '90	TAPE ALBUM: 10 GROUP SERIES (77.50)	
SPECIAL SUBJECTS: AB-			
GROUP SERIES: G-			
	(If you need more space, add another sheet of paper)		

(S/H) SHIPPING & HANDLING RATES Continental U.S.A.	
Up to $10.00 . . . . . . add $2.75	**ADD TOTAL OF ITEMS** _____
10.00 to 30.00 . . . . . .add 3.90	**ADD SHIPPING & HANDLING** _____
30.00 to 50.00 . . . . . .add 5.40	(Subtract any quantity discounts) _____
Over 50.00 . . . . .add 6.70	(TX delivery, add 6.25% Sales Tax) _____
	(Add/subtract credits or chgs) _____
	TOTAL AMOUNT ENCLOSED _____

[ ] PERSONAL CHECK (Make checks payable to: J & E Hicks)
[ ] MASTERCARD   [ ] VISA   [ ] OTHER

CARD #_____EXP DATE_____

NAME ON CARD (PRINT)_____

CARDHOLDER'S SIGNATURE_____

THANK YOU!

Our thanks to you for your role in this joyous cocreation. Your thoughts as we interact, your pondering, questioning, recognizing, knowing, wanting...your thoughts add to our forward motion and to the fulfillment of our purpose.

We intend to allow Abrahams' words of perspective, positive guidance, and stimulation of thought, to go as far and as fast as they are wanted, and at the same time, we intend to continue our abundant positive mental and material and spiritual experience — and we do appreciate your contribution of "thoughts, words and deeds."

Do you have a friend who would enjoy our newsletter?

Name (Please print)_____

Address_____

City/State/Zip_____

Do you participate with a progressive group? Would you like to engage Abraham & Esther & Jerry for a weekend or a workshop for your group? If so, we would like to hear from you. Comments:

YOUR UNCONDITIONAL
GUARANTEE OF SATISFACTION

We are aware that due to technical or personal idiosyncrasys you may receive a damaged or defective item from us — but we will replace it or refund your money (whichever you prefer) just as soon as you call or write and give us the details. Please don't bother with shipping the item back to us. Just toss it away. We want you to be completely satisfied with our products and our service.

Jerry & Esther

ORDER FORM
FILL OUT AND CALL IT IN TO: (512) 755-2299
After Nov., 1992 Area Code changes to (210)
OR MAIL TO: ABRAHAM SPEAKS
P.O. BOX 1706, BOERNE, TX 78006

NAME (Please print)_____

ADDRESS_____

CITY_____STATE_____

ZIP_____TEL._____

(To ship by UPS, we need your street or R.R. number—not a P.O box)

QUANTITY	STOCK NUMBER	ITEM	PRICE
	AB-1	TAPE: FREE INTRO TO ABRAHAM (S/H ONLY)	2.75
	ANBI	BOOK: "A NEW BEGINNING I" (@ 9.95)	
	ANBII	BOOK: "A NEW BEGINNING II" (@ 9.95)	
	VOL I	TAPE ALBUM: 10 SPECIAL SUBJECTS (77.50)	
	VOL II	TAPE ALBUM: 10 SPECIAL SUBJECTS (77.50)	
	G-SUMMER '90	TAPE ALBUM: 10 GROUP SERIES (77.50)	
SPECIAL SUBJECTS: AB-			
GROUP SERIES: G-			
(If you need more space, add another sheet of paper)			

(S/H) SHIPPING & HANDLING RATES Continental U.S.A.	
Up to $10.00 . . . . . . add $2.75	
10.00 to 30.00 . . . . . .add 3.90	
30.00 to 50.00 . . . . . .add 5.40	
Over 50.00 . . . . add 6.70	

ADD TOTAL OF ITEMS	
ADD SHIPPING & HANDLING	
(Subtract any quantity discounts)	
(TX delivery, add 6.25% Sales Tax)	
(Add/subtract credits or chgs)	
TOTAL AMOUNT ENCLOSED	

[ ] PERSONAL CHECK (Make checks payable to: J & E Hicks)

[ ] MASTERCARD   [ ] VISA   [ ] OTHER

CARD #_____EXP DATE_____

NAME ON CARD (PRINT)_____

CARDHOLDER'S SIGNATURE_____

Pioneers 123

THANK YOU!

Our thanks to you for your role in this joyous cocreation. Your thoughts as we interact, your pondering, questioning, recognizing, knowing, wanting...your thoughts add to our forward motion and to the fulfillment of our purpose.

We intend to allow Abrahams' words of perspective, positive guidance, and stimulation of thought, to go as far and as fast as they are wanted, and at the same time, we intend to continue our abundant positive mental and material and spiritual experience — and we do appreciate your contribution of "thoughts, words and deeds."

Do you have a friend who would enjoy our newsletter?

Name (Please print)_____
Address_____
City/State/Zip_____

Do you participate with a progressive group? Would you like to engage Abraham & Esther & Jerry for a weekend or a workshop for your group? If so, we would like to hear from you. Comments:

YOUR UNCONDITIONAL
GUARANTEE OF SATISFACTION

We are aware that due to technical or personal idiosyncrasys you may receive a damaged or defective item from us — but we will replace it or refund your money (whichever you prefer) just as soon as you call or write and give us the details. Please don't bother with shipping the item back to us. Just toss it away. We want you to be completely satisfied with our products and our service.

Jerry & Esther